ADVANCE PRAISE FOR
BEYOND THE MAT

"Dr. Rosenberg has the courage to make the connections between mind, body, productivity, and authenticity. In a cynical world full of self-doubt and fear of the future, Rosenberg presents a way through the commotion and noise that is practical, applicable, and designed to allow us to live more congruent, purposeful lives. It's one thing to talk in platitudes. It's another thing to embrace an approach that increases the probability we will live the kind of lives that we dream about."

—PROFESSOR THOMAS DELONG, senior fellow and former professor of Organizational Behavior at Harvard Business School and former head of Human Capital at Morgan Stanley

"Dr. Julie Rosenberg's *Beyond the Mat* urges readers to use yoga to improve their lives in and beyond the workplace and demonstrates the potential power of yoga to transform lives, systems, and organizations. The book is an important contribution to a body of literature that celebrates and cultivates compassion, kindness, and empathy."

—DR. BARBARA VACARR, CEO of Kripalu Center for Yoga & Health

"With a lovely candor and pragmatism, Julie Rosenberg explores how applying yoga practices can transform both the personal and the corporate landscape. Read *Beyond the Mat* for insight into essential yogic principles, as well as simple and inspiring lessons on how to integrate them into daily life. A vital contribution for anyone trying to bring their best self into the workplace."

—NATASHA RIZOPOULOS, master teacher and teacher trainer; creator of Align Your Flow™

"Dr. Rosenberg's book examines the internal process of improving mindfulness through the principles and practices of yoga. As someone who has gained great insight through my own practice of mindfulness, the concepts and ideas outlined in this book are highly relevant to anyone working to achieve greater focus, presence, and enlightened leadership."

—MARK BERTOLINI, chairman and CEO, Aetna

"*Beyond the Mat* serves as a compass for leaders to work and breathe with purpose beyond traditional markers of success. Weaving between easy step-by-step handbook and stories of real-life experiences, Julie Rosenberg offers both path and parable for anyone who hopes to lead by service and clarity of vision and intention. This wonderful book provides a chance to detach from the distractions of 'business book' a leadership and anchor to the precepts of human leadership. *Beyond the Mat* is my new desktop companion, and I am certain it will serve my company, my employees, and me quite well."

—STANTON KAWER, chairman and CEO, Blue Chip Marketing
Worldwide

"Dr. Rosenberg combines the rare talents of advanced medical training and practice, leadership in a high pressure industry, and hundreds of hours of training in yoga and meditation to share with us the 'special sauce' and power of success: a practice of yoga that combines mind, body, and spirit. Her tools, even as simple as twisting in your chair purposefully at work, will enhance your life and will be used to coach my patients in my clinic."

—JOEL K. KAHN, MD, FACC, clinical professor of cardiology;
author, *The Whole Heart Solution*

"Offering easily accessible and concise practices for body and mind, Julie Rosenberg captures the depth and wisdom of ancient yoga in the every-day tools she presents in *Beyond the Mat*. I am always on the hunt for a book that inspires both my students and me—Dr. Rosenberg gives everyone the tools necessary to walk through personal and professional life with embodiment, peace, and precision."

—JENNIFER REIS, certified yoga therapist and faculty, Kripalu
School of Yoga and Creator of Divine Sleep Yoga Nidra®

"Many of us are struggling with busyness, stress, and exhaustion in the face of our over-burdening lives and over-demanding roles. What Julie Rosenberg does beautifully in this book is to apply the ancient wisdom of yoga to the modern challenges of twenty-first-century life and work. This book is both practical and profound. It's like a new set of glasses: it helps you to see familiar problems a bit differently, a bit more clearly. It also provides a host of simple techniques and tools to respond more effectively. For anyone who has found mindfulness useful, this book is a must; it will help you extend your mindfulness through your body, life, and leadership."

—TONY CRABBE, author of *Busy: How to Thrive in a World of Too Much*

"*Beyond the Mat* unrolls the red carpet of yoga in front of the reader—it demystifies yoga and makes the practices of mindfulness, pranayama, and asanas accessible to every reader. Dr. Julie Rosenberg shares her personal experience as to how practicing these techniques can help with stress management, job performance, and personal satisfaction. Everyone wants to feel good, and to feel good about themselves. *Beyond the Mat* offers a sound practice of how to achieve both."

—MARK LIPONIS, MD, chief medical officer, Canyon Ranch, and author of *Ultralongevity* and *The Hunter Farmer Diet Solution*

"Full of user-friendly tools that make yoga accessible for even the busiest and most skeptical, Julie Rosenberg's *Beyond the Mat* is an intelligent and easy-to-read practical guide to life for everyone. Julie's own personal journey and experience offer a captivating backdrop and give her words of wisdom great credence. Inspiring!"

—JURIAN HUGHES, E-RYT 500, MFA, Kripalu School of Yoga, senior faculty

"It is time for a book like this one! Julie Rosenberg is an authentic voice for the integration of yoga philosophy and leadership skills. Her personal experience in yoga and corporate America, upfront honesty, and practicality combine to create a book that is as useful as it is inspirational."

—KATE O'DONNELL, author of *The Everyday Ayurveda Cookbook* and *Everyday Ayurveda Cooking for a Calm, Clear Mind*

"*Beyond the Mat* achieves something more important than hope and more practical than inspiration: with every page it demonstrates the concrete, life-changing efficacy of yoga and meditation. This timely book shows us how to become the dynamic and positively impactful leaders we want to be, and the world needs us to be, one breath and one moment at a time."

—SEAN MESHORER, author of *The Bliss Experiment*

"Dr. Rosenberg has done an excellent job combining the hard science of the medical profession with the soft science of mindfulness in a beautiful way. The messages offer insights that, when practiced, will lead to a healthier life—mentally, physically, emotionally, and spiritually."

—MARSHA CLARK, CEO, Marsha Clark & Associates

"Bravo! Dr. Julie Rosenberg beautifully articulates the vast, complex benefits of the yoga practice in a way that is consumable and deeply relevant to the modern, fast-paced lifestyle that challenges so many of us on a daily basis."

—BEN CHUSED, yoga instructor and teacher trainer

"Powerful and important. When businesses bring yoga into the workplace, they usually do so to improve team wellness. Dr. Rosenberg's convincing and important book shows that they should also do so to improve team leadership. A necessary read for the corporate and business world."

—MICHAEL ELLSBERG, author of *The Education of Millionaires* and co-author of *The Last Safe Investment*

"An insightful reminder that yoga has so much more to offer than just poses. *Beyond the Mat* offers a powerful journey of holistic leadership principles by walking the reader through the eight limbs of Ashtanga and how they relate to enlightened leadership and personal transformation. An excellent read for all."

—CHARLY KLEISSNER, Ph.D., co-founder Toniic, 100% Impact Network, KL Felicitas Foundation

Beyond the Mat

Beyond the Mat

ACHIEVE FOCUS, PRESENCE,
and ENLIGHTENED LEADERSHIP
through the Principles and Practice of Yoga

Julie Rosenberg, MD

Da Capo

LIFE
LONG

Da Capo Press
Hachette Book Group
53 State Street, Boston, MA 02109
www.dacapopress.com
@dacapopress

Printed in the United States of America
First Edition: December 2017
Published by Da Capo Press, an imprint of Perseus Books, LLC,
a subsidiary of Hachette Book Group, Inc.
The publisher is not responsible for websites (or their content)
that are not owned by the publisher.

All illustrations © 2017 Samantha Hahn.
Author photo on page 239 by Vanessa Joy Photography.
Editorial support by Claire Schulz at Da Capo Press.
Editorial production by Lori Hobkirk at the Book Factory.
Print book interior design by Cynthia Young at Sagecraft.

Library of Congress Cataloging-in-Publication Data has been applied for.
ISBN: 978-0-7382-1960-8
E-book ISBN: 978-0-7382-1985-1
LCCN: 2017956461

LSC-C

10 9 8 7 6 5 4 3 2 1

In memoriam
William Jay Katz

To my father,
who taught me to stand on my own two feet
and to appreciate the power of the written word.

Contents

Introduction

Our team faced its biggest challenge of the year: a high-stakes presentation to senior management about a pivotal clinical trial for a new type of cancer treatment.

We had prepared and practiced tirelessly for months—convening teleconferences and web meetings to connect the thirty-five-person team from their offices across the United States and Europe. Now the big day was here. My colleague Jim and I met in our New York City office and ascended to the twenty-fifth floor to deliver a presentation to twenty top leaders in the company. In a matter of hours we would request funding to proceed to a phase-three clinical trial, where our new drug would be evaluated in a large group of patients to confirm its effectiveness, identify side effects, and compare its effectiveness to an existing treatment.

Sure, things looked promising—the numbers were good, and our earlier clinical trials had gone well. If the plans for the phase-three trial were approved by management, successfully conducted, and concluded as anticipated, we would be ready to submit our application to regulators worldwide with the ultimate goal of marketing a drug that would allow more patients access to a desperately needed anticancer agent.

We needed to positively influence the most senior executives in our company to support this final phase of the program; funding goes to those programs deemed to have the best odds of success. This meant securing enough money to conduct a phase-three trial. A quarter of a billion dollars would do.

Welcome to the world of pharmaceuticals. High stakes and high pressure. Lives and profits continually in the balance. In the midst of this pressure I felt reasonably calm and self-assured. My boss had often suggested that I am too matter-of-fact. In reality my temperament is anything but matter-of-fact because I know that there is so much more than money at stake. If we failed to make our case, a potentially life-saving treatment for millions of people could get held up indefinitely. Further, our team's investment in this program could come to a screeching halt, and those of us working on the team would need to scramble for other positions both within the company and beyond. Demands in the industry are continually high, and circumstances can shift at a moment's notice. So I often pondered how to best cope with the stress of my job.

I am a pediatric oncologist who has worked in the field of oncology for nearly two decades. I am intimately familiar with why these drugs are necessary and what can happen when an effective agent is unnecessarily delayed due to bureaucratic red tape. So when I said this was a high-stakes presentation, I meant it. It was not only high-stakes, it was also highly personal.

I come from a "cancer family." Most everyone on my father's side of my family has had cancer, and the majority ultimately succumbed to disease. My father, a very fit athlete even into his later years, died in a frail condition six months after a diagnosis of advanced kidney cancer. My sister has lived with chronic myelogenous leukemia (CML) for the past seven years. Interestingly, her primary treatment has been with dasatinib, a drug that I worked to evaluate in children with CML prior to and during the time of her diagnosis. This was a surreal experience—there are only about fifty-five hundred new cases of CML diagnosed per year (that's rare!), mostly in the elderly, and my forty-eight-year-old sister was diagnosed with the very disease that I was then studying in children.

I too am a cancer survivor. I am a twenty-four-year survivor of stage-one papillary carcinoma of the thyroid. Although I no longer fear dying from this disease, I suffer from dry mouth, dry eyes, and intermittent hoarseness of voice from the complications of surgery and subsequent treatment with radioactive iodine. These symptoms are chronic, and I am reminded daily of my disease as I attempt to live a "normal" life. These reminders are often subtle, such as the need to frequently use eye drops, but they are, nevertheless, reminders. As more and more information has become available about cancer survivorship and the risk of second cancers, I sometimes worry about what's next for me. However, I have decided not to have genetic testing to ascertain my future risk of certain other cancers. I prefer to limit my stress and anxiety around the diagnostic possibilities that may arise based on these past circumstances. All I can control are my lifestyle choices. One of my choices is yoga.

Believe it or not, I have found that my yoga practice is the answer to coping with stress, both in my personal life and on the job. As I was about to deliver this key presentation I felt calm. Jim, however, was anxious and sweating. His nervousness was palpable. Why the difference? I had learned through my yoga practice to stand tall with an open posture, to breathe though anxiety, and to stay focused on the task at hand. I was not fearful, but rather I embraced this challenging situation with high risk, as I knew I could grow from it.

Supervising a large global drug development program is incredibly challenging, but it offers me the opportunity to help develop new drugs that will serve cancer patients worldwide. And for the past fifteen years the millennia-old physical, mental, and spiritual discipline of yoga has made it possible for me: healing my body by enhancing my ability to handle stress and anxiety and building my resilience, agility, and stamina—thus strengthening my leadership capacity and capability. Yoga has been so effective in enhancing my own life, both at work and at home, that I decided to become certified as an instructor so I could share this passion with others. Since 2012 I have taught others how to thrive through yoga by embodying its principles both on and beyond the mat—the ultimate goal.

Most of us think of this ancient, mind-body, Indian-born tradition as a fitness hobby, a gentler alternative to trendy options like SoulCycle or CrossFit, useful for those of us, mostly women, often professional, looking to relieve stress and fight time's effect on our bodies.

But my experience as a leader operating at a high level in corporate America has shown me that yoga—both its physically challenging asanas (postures) and its profound, far-reaching philosophy—is a rich, robust technology for personal and professional development. All you need to begin is a willingness to engage and possibly a yoga mat. You can even do plenty at your desk. It won't freak out your coworkers (they will want to do it too).

Yoga is my secret weapon. My personal practice—typically thirty minutes or less each morning—gives me the strength, poise, flexibility, and groundedness to lead with confidence in demanding environments where mistakes cost lives and fortunes.

Senior management at my company is infamous for derailing teams—presenters are rarely able to complete their presentations in the face of an endless barrage of interruptions.

The day prior to this high-stakes presentation we spent the morning reviewing the slides and agreeing on key discussion points. I knew we were ready to go, but the team kept evaluating and re-evaluating its decision making. At this stage the team members were just adding to their own anxiety. It wasn't helping any of us to feel more prepared.

Try This in Two Minutes

Twist in a Chair to Free Your Achy Back

In the workplace many of us spend the majority of our day sitting at our desks with our shoulders tense and upper backs gripping. When we get up and walk away, we carry our tension with us. This simple movement, a seated twist, will stimulate circulation to your spine, alleviate tense back muscles, and help increase mental focus. It is a great pose to do before a big meeting or presentation, as it can relax your back muscles, help to dissolve anxiety, and allow you to become less tense and better focused. It's also a great pose to use midflight during air travel or anytime you have to sit for long periods of time. A seated twist will help an achy back from hunching when sitting and supports all-around good posture.

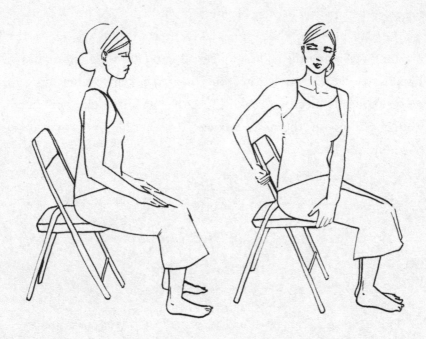

Seated Twist

Sit in your chair with your spine tall and straight, keeping both feet on the floor and your knees facing forward. Take a deep inhale. On the exhale twist to one side from the bottom of your spine, engaging your abdomen and rolling your shoulder blades back and down while gently grabbing the side of the chair that you're twisted toward. Keep your chin lined up with the center of your chest. Breathe here for five to eight breaths, seeing if you can grow your spine longer with each inhalation and can deepen the twist with each exhalation. After five to eight breaths, return to center and do the other side.

Reflecting on what I've learned in more than a decade of yoga practice I took several deep, grounding breaths, reviewed the slides one last time to ensure that there were no remaining considerations, and left.

Rather than dwell on the challenge ahead, I decided to invest my energy in some needed self-care. I went to a sushi bar for lunch. Then, on the spur of the moment, I bought a ticket to a Broadway show. I had a seat in the third row, and the play was terrific. I left the theater feeling refreshed and rejuvenated, and I returned to my hotel room and got a good night's sleep.

The next morning was our big day. I woke at 5:00 a.m. as usual. Then I went to the gym. I sat on a stool in the back of the locker room—the gym is not too busy at that hour—and meditated for a few minutes. Yogic mediation has helped me to expand my conscious awareness and has given me more freedom and empowerment in my life. Then I ran on the treadmill for a half hour, focusing on keeping a slow, even breathing pattern and clearing my mind. I don't typically run with headphones while listening to music, as I appreciate the quietude and being disengaged from noise for a while. I concluded my time at the gym with a twenty-minute asana practice, again focusing on my breath to support the movements—inhale, exhale, inhale, exhale. I left feeling open, light, and awake.

After my morning yoga practice I showered, got dressed in a well-tailored power suit, and ate a healthy breakfast (yes, these things—personal presence and good nutrition—are part of living your yoga practice, as you'll find in the coming pages). I walked over to the office, ready to take on the management team. I was confident, alert, and poised.

My colleagues and I entered the conference room. There were no name cards in front of the twenty members of the senior leadership team, and I knew only a few. I greeted those nearest me and sat with no trepidation at the head of the table.

All eyes were on us. After a pause the head of our program spoke first. Her anxiety was palpable; she failed to even introduce the two of us responsible for delivering the presentation on behalf of the team.

Great, I thought. *Here I am, a relative unknown trying to get a room full of strangers to give me lots of money. And I can't even get introduced properly.*

Luckily the time I'd spent on my yoga practice that morning and for so many mornings before it helped me side-step that flare of annoyance and stay in the moment. Jim began the discussion. After he finished speaking I paused, took a deep breath, and then continued the proceedings with confidence. I knew that we "owned" the room. This was "our day."

After all, the senior management team and I were equals as human beings. We were on the same team. We had the same goal of serving patients while supporting the needs of the corporation. Looking through eyes clarified by the philosophy and practice of yoga instead of seeing the management team as "them," I saw "us," a room full of allies and friends.

I explained the issues at hand, the options on the table, the plan we had in mind, and the choice we thought they should make. No one interrupted me. When I finished you could hear a pin drop in the room. Silence. Engagement. They were thinking about what they'd heard.

It typically takes twenty-four to forty-eight hours for management to decide on program funding. And yet I felt no surprise twenty minutes after the discussion had concluded when we received the green light.

It was the fastest funding decision any of us had ever seen at the company.

Yoga continues to enhance my effectiveness as a leader—the discipline, the community, and the practice have helped me to become more engaged at work and to better manage my team. As a leader I focus not only on results but also on people, their individual needs, and how to help them recognize their individual and collective value to the success of the organization. Yoga has helped me ensure that I don't take things too personally, that I can accept the wins and the losses with detachment and with the same grace and ease. I have developed an intuitive sense of my strengths as a negotiator and an influencer. I am better able to let things go and to move forward through success and failure, keeping both at the proper size and proportion.

Yoga, writes Mahadev Desai in his introduction to *The Bhagavad Gita According to Gandhi*, "enables one to look at life in all its aspects evenly."

Our Western view of yoga is that it is a discipline composed of a series of pretzel-like physical exertions done to get fit and flexible, usually with some token Sanskrit words thrown in here and there to keep things interesting but somewhat elusive. Yoga is also an industry, one worth billions of dollars each year: the market is rife with swanky supplies and trendy clothing as well as exclusive yoga retreats in exotic places. A 2016 Yoga in America study showed that annual practitioner spending on yoga classes, clothing, equipment, and accessories rose to $16 billion, up from $10 billion over the past four years.

Yoga is now promoted for nearly everything—from helping people recover from injuries, to reducing anxiety and depression, to aiding practitioners in staying toned and fit. I read recently that I can better bond with my dog through *doga*—yes, that's yoga with your dog. Don't have a dog? Never fear. A cat shelter outside of Atlanta hosted a yoga class with felines; it was a great hit! Live in a rural area? Forget Downward Facing Dog—try Downward Facing Goat! Classes are popping up all around the country that actually include yoga alongside farm animals. It often seems like everybody and their mother (or brother) is either practicing yoga or planning to change careers and training to become a certified yoga instructor.

But at its heart yoga is neither fashion nor fitness (and, as fun as doga may sound, yoga is not meant as an avenue to bond with our pets!). What most people refer to as *yoga* is but one aspect (asana, or "postures") of a much larger, interconnected system. Along with the postures comes breathwork, concentration, observances, withdrawal, restraints, and meditation—all components of the complete practice. Yoga is a practical philosophy of self-observation and inner inquiry. The concept of self-awareness or knowing oneself is central to both yoga and leadership.

My study and practice of yoga have greatly impacted my understanding of leadership and how I lead. The purpose of this book is to distill the essential lessons of the yoga sutras into a meaningful framework for leaders at all levels. The yoga sutras, despite being at least four thousand years old, are as relevant today as they were in ancient India. They offer ways in which you as a leader can bring greater focus, clarity, and self-awareness to your leadership approach. My goal is to help you to change the way you think in order to change the way you act. The good news: if you practice yoga or want to start a practice, that's great! Even if you think yoga is not for you, keep reading. You don't need to be an ardent yoga practitioner to understand and implement this framework. Why? Yoga tells us that we are our own best teacher or guru. This book provides you with structure, support, instruction, and encouragement. When you can define what leadership means to you and use your learnings to support your evolution as a leader, you will not only be more self-aware and present for your life, but you will also communicate more effectively and better influence those whom you lead.

The eight limbs of Ashtanga yoga map the journey one takes when studying and practicing yoga. The eight limbs support an aspirant in drawing his or her consciousness from an external focus to an internal focus. The Yoga Sutras of Patañjali are the 196 Indian sutras, or aphorisms, that the Hindu scholar Patañjali compiled from even older traditions. The right means are as important as the end goal, according to Patañjali. He enumerates these means as the eight limbs, or stages of yoga for the quest of the soul:

1. *Yama* (universal moral commandments)

2. *Niyama* (self-purification by discipline)

3. *Asana* (posture)

4. *Pranayama* (rhythmic control of breath)

5. *Pratyahara* (withdrawal and liberation of the mind from the domination of the senses and exterior objects)

6. *Dharana* (concentration)

7. *Dhyana* (meditation)

8. *Samadhi* (the highest stage in meditation, in which a person experiences oneness with the universe)

This book is organized in the same order as the eight limbs. In the following chapters I will lead you through the steps to developing a yoga mindset of your own that will help you lead yourself and others in a more effective and sustainable way, one that brings you joy and bliss in your life and work. By reading and assimilating the content of this book you are beginning a journey into a world of profound wisdom and sage advice that will transform you as a person and a leader. It will unlock your professional potential. It will reduce stress. It will increase your happiness at work and in your personal life.

People will start asking you what you're doing to achieve the obvious change in attitude and demeanor—they're going to want to know your secret.

The following pages will give you the tools, knowledge, and inspiration to transform your life and improve your overall satisfaction at home and at work.

1

Laying the
Foundation for Success

"Waste no more time arguing about what a good
man should be. Be one."

—Marcus Aurelius, *Meditations*

Very few of us arise in the morning excited about the workday ahead.
There may even be days when we just can't bear to get out of bed to go
to work. Many of us hate our jobs, our long hours, and, especially, our
boss. We lack autonomy, and we don't feel in control.

If this sounds familiar, know that it's not just you. Burnout is a
growing problem in businesses everywhere. Workplace burnout is more
than just fatigue, and it goes beyond having a bad day, a bad week, or
even a bad month. The term burnout was coined by psychologist Herbert Freudenberger in 1974, referring to "the extinction of motivation
or incentive, especially where one's devotion to a cause or relationship
fails to produce the desired results." Burnout is characterized by a
chronic state of emotional and physical exhaustion as well as strong

feelings of frustration and powerlessness. Those suffering from work-place burnout tend to withdraw emotionally from their work, lose mo-tivation, and become less productive.

Feelings of burnout go well beyond the workplace and may impact our everyday lives. Have you ever felt like you've had the life sucked out of you, like you seem to have lost your ability to care about anything and everything, to make an effort, and to find positive motivation? Most of us have been there—and that's burnout.

Furthermore, we work too much. The need to be on call 24/7 and to work six or even seven days per week is no longer restricted to high-level professionals such as physicians, lawyers, and business executives. In our modern, global corporate environment, to meet our company's cross-cultural needs, employees in many functional areas are expected to have such availability.

This is what management worries about: employee satisfaction and retention. Costly churn can be devastating for corporations. Satisfied employees feel a connection to the organization's mission, purpose, and leadership. How can we get there?

Believe it or not, yoga is a solution to improved employee satisfac-tion, workplace happiness, stress reduction, and productivity. Studying and adopting the philosophical underpinnings of yoga allow for a greater sense of overall stability despite external distractions, and incor-porating yogic breathing and postures to unify and relax the mind and body provides an ongoing framework in which to manage workplace stress and uncertainty.

Using these techniques provides a way to quietly and unobtrusively cope with the crises that occur during the day. Practicing yoga has been found to reduce pain, relieve tension, decrease risks of injury, improve posture and communication, increase energy and attention span, and bring about feelings of overall well-being.

Too many people talk about a company's leadership, referring to the senior-most executives in the organization. Leadership has nothing to do with titles, whether you have a corner office, or where you sit at the conference table. Inherently, defining leadership means understanding yourself from an inward perspective as well as translating your own tendencies, strengths, and approaches into the way you interact, communicate, and influence others. To me, leadership is the collective action of everyone I influence. My behavior—both actions and words—determines how I influence. My job as a leader is to use my personal power to encourage, inspire, and energize others to action.

Successful leadership isn't about what you know; it's about who you are and how you show up. Behavior can change, and leaders who work to improve their skills generally get results.

So how can you more clearly define the foundations of what it will take for you to become a successful leader? Can an understanding of yoga help you better comprehend what makes certain leaders more effective than others, and if so, how you can implement those skills yourself?

Buddhism swept across the United States starting in the late 1960s and has dominated the conversation around non-Western spirituality ever since. Yoga is just as broad a philosophy/belief system as Buddhism but is still narrowly viewed by many in the United States as a physical fitness practice. And there are many different offerings—variants of yoga such as rock-and-roll yoga, hip-hop yoga, yoga fusion, naked yoga, aerial yoga, acroyoga, and more. Although the physical practice of each of these varies greatly, they all stem from a millennia-old tradition of action, self-knowledge, and wisdom.

Yoga has significant philosophical roots, many of which intersect on a secular level with Buddhism. (One intersection of yoga and Buddhism is that both promote a sense of mindfulness—the ability to be fully present in the moment, to be aware of bodily sensations and breath, to suspend judgment and to simply be aware of passing thoughts and emotions. Mindfulness practice helps us to detach our minds from pursuing desires or avoiding displeasures.)

The first of the eight limbs of yoga are the *yamas*, universal moral and ethical commandments for "right living." They are guidelines for how we can best show up for our lives, and they apply broadly to our actions, words, and thoughts. I have come to see the yamas as an essential foundation for success in life, personally and professionally—and the basis of effective leadership, no matter what your job description entails.

The yamas are broken down into five "wise characteristics." On the surface these five wise characteristics may sound familiar to those of us in the West: don't commit violence (ahimsa), tell the truth (satya), don't steal what others have (asteya), practice self-restraint (brahmacharya), and take only what is necessary (aparigraha). But unlike our more commonly understood set of rules, the Ten Commandments, the yamas go deeper as rules of morality for society and individuals. Rather than a list of dos and don'ts, the yamas aim to help practitioners develop a powerful set of interpersonal skills, from patience to fearlessness.

Ahimsa

Ahimsa literally means not to injure or show cruelty to any living being. However, as adopted in yoga practice and in life beyond the mat, ahimsa is much more than the literal interpretation of nonviolence; it

The Yamas

Ahimsa—nonviolence/compassion

Satya—truth

Asteya—nonstealing

Brahmacharya—control of the senses

Aparigraha—to take only what is necessary

implies that in every situation we should adopt a kind, thoughtful, and considerate attitude and that we should also exercise compassion.

In the early years of our careers we are measured primarily for our individual contributions. Thus, it is often difficult for emerging leaders to recognize that leadership is not solely about them and their ability to attract and direct followers; it is about serving others to bring out the best in the collective group. How else can leaders unleash the power of their organizations unless they motivate people to reach their full potential? If our supporters are merely following our lead, then their efforts are limited to our vision and our directions. Only when leaders stop focusing on their personal ego needs are they able to develop others. This is how ahimsa—compassion and kindness—makes a leader truly effective and is a first step on the path to enlightened leadership.

I was guilty of the "I syndrome" earlier in my career. Although my intent was pure—I wanted to be a vital force in advancing global health and wellness—I was too focused on my own success. I too often compared myself to others, and rather than support and promote them, I wanted to surpass them to more rapidly advance toward my goals.

I also was never satisfied with my present circumstance or the "status quo" and wanted more in terms of opportunity—which I thought could be accomplished by rapidly advancing my rank.

I was wrong. In essence, such behavior served to hold me back by alienating the people I needed to support my desire to more expansive leadership. With the help of a good coach I learned. My coach gave me a proverbial "slap in the face," which helped me to shift my thinking and behaviors so I became less focused on myself and more engaged with my team. I now understand that it's critical to cultivate, maintain, and nurture business relationships, and although I'm still focused on my own success, making sure members of my team are also supported and positioned to realize their own potential is even more critical to me. I realize that in addition to offering my expertise and guidance, my team members want to feel that I respect them, care about them, and that I'll do whatever it takes to help them. I do and I will.

Look in the mirror. Who are you? Why are you here? What is your life purpose?

Have you thought about these things? Be honest. Once you have a true understanding of yourself, you can gain a better understanding of others and create more effective relationships. The Tibetan scholar Thupten Jinpa, longtime English translator for the Dalai Lama, defines compassion as having three components: (1) a cognitive component: "I understand you"; (2) an affective component: "I feel for you"; and (3) a motivational component: "I want to help you." The practice of compassion is about going from self to others. To become a highly effective leader you must go through an important transformation from focusing on yourself to focusing on others. Bill George, in *Discover Your True North*, puts it most succinctly: This shift is the transformation from "I" to "We."

Compassion Matters

A new colleague, Leslie, joined my team and seemed somewhat slow to grasp concepts and ideas at a time when the team was extremely burdened by deliverables with tight deadlines. I spent several hours trying to orient her to the program, but my efforts seemed to no avail. She remained inept in my view, and we needed a highly functional team member *now*. We were at a critical crossroads in our program.

I spoke to her manager regarding her initial poor performance and then moved on to focus on key deliverables. But in that time period I failed to exercise ahimsa; I was so frustrated that I "delegated" the situation to her manager and, in the ensuing days, proceeded ahead with other business that I deemed to be more important than fostering a relationship with Leslie.

Despite my initial mistake I reflected on my behavior. Reflection is critical to enhance self-awareness and often the first key to change. I realized that my task as a leader was to exercise compassion and let go of this overt frustration. I quickly reassessed the situation and enlisted broader support for Leslie, including my own. She was new to the role, the team, and the program—perhaps I had expected too much of her in the initial weeks. Once I let go of my quick judgments and offered more compassionate, constructive guidance, things turned around quickly both for Leslie and our team. Gradually Leslie became more comfortable and effective in her role, and the team became more cohesive.

The most compelling professional benefits of compassion are that it engages employees by building an inspired workforce, and it creates highly effective leaders. The core of compassion is suspending judgment in order to have an appreciation of others' perspectives when they are different from your own. Compassionate individuals are genuinely concerned about other people and their needs. When others are suffering, they take action to help relieve it. Compassionate leaders strive to create emotionally healthy and positively energized workplaces that support good morale and enhanced employee engagement and productivity. They have a people-centered approach, with a focus on connection and collaboration. Compassionate leaders genuinely care for the well-being of others and are attentive to their needs, which they put before their own.

Managers often mistakenly think that putting high pressure on employees will improve their performance. But what it actually does is increase stress and anxiety. Compassion in the workplace is effective for building trust, which leads to loyalty and employee retention. Feelings of warmth and positive relationships at work also enhance employee productivity and efficiency.

Organizations that foster compassion typically measure overall success in terms of team or collective success rather than individual success. A culture of compassion has been positively correlated with employee wellness, job satisfaction, commitment to the company, and accountability for performance. All of these things can translate into lower levels of turnover and an improved financial bottom line.

Stop to ask yourself: Am I satisfied with my job?

Job satisfaction is a big component of employee engagement. There are a variety of characteristics that influence job satisfaction, such as (1) job responsibilities (the more varied tasks are, the higher the satisfaction), (2) leadership (leaders who give recognition and praise and who

Try This in Two Minutes

Think about your job and ponder these questions. Is your management concerned about the emotional culture at work? How does your boss treat you when she sees you? How do you greet your colleagues and subordinates? How does your typical day at the office begin? Do you run into your office to a barrage of work-related emails from impatient colleagues and clients who want them answered *now*? Or do you exchange a series of greetings with coworkers or perhaps grab a quick cup of coffee before the daily work deluge begins? How do you feel at the start of your day? Do these early feelings correlate with how you experience the remainder of your day? What can you do to either sustain positive feelings or to ensure that your day begins on a more positive note?

consider the opinions of employees generate higher levels of satisfaction), (3) pay and opportunity for advancement (both directly associated with satisfaction), and (4) respect from bosses and coworkers (a community in which managers and coworkers respect each other supports good morale).

Although much has been written about this topic, I would like to focus on one of the key components of job satisfaction: autonomy. Autonomy in the workplace refers to how much freedom and opportunity for self-direction employees have in their work environment. For most of us it's important to believe that we have choices, that we are the source of our own actions and decision making, and that we want to take ownership for our work. Studies have shown that autonomy is associated with greater job satisfaction and increased productivity.

Autonomy is particularly critical when it comes to creating and maintaining our sense of intrinsic motivation—doing something for the pure enjoyment or fun of it rather than for a reward. As a leader I have seen many people, including myself, feel disempowered at work. We are constantly fielding requests and taking orders, struggling to meet the demands and expectations of our superiors who then pass judgment on our work.

Jim Goodnight, cofounder and CEO of SAS, the world's leading business analytics software vendor, is an example of a compassionate leader who supports employee autonomy. The forty-year old software company has not just survived the tumultuous changes in the technology industry but has thrived, posting steady growth year after year. Goodnight, who has led the company since its inception in 1976, holds employees in high esteem and has often said that the secret to the success of SAS is taking care of employees—helping them grow and giving them high levels of autonomy.

When leaders care about employees and are committed to supporting their professional growth and development, they are more likely to offer them high levels of autonomy. Such leaders are also more likely to acknowledge out-of-the-box ideas that come from their team, and they don't take the credit themselves. An environment that promotes creative thinking and a constant exchange of ideas along with individual autonomy and group collaboration supports innovation.

Earlier I mentioned that it's important for leaders to move from an "I" to a "we" focus. But compassion for others is just one side of the coin. Cultivating compassion for yourself is one of the toughest tasks for a leader, both professionally and personally. You might not need to look far to find an example of self-critical talk or a lack of compassion for yourself. For instance, I am a mom who thinks that motherhood is

Since its founding Google has been committed to active philanthropy and addressing the global challenges of climate change, education, and alleviating poverty. Chade-Meng Tan, an early Google employee, personal growth pioneer, and best-selling author, has described Google as a company born out of idealism, at which compassion is organic and widespread throughout the company. Googlers from around the world are encouraged to donate their skills and labor to support service projects in their local communities. The compassionate environment at Google has led to a culture of passionate concern for the greater good, high levels of autonomy, and a corporate focus on personal growth and development.

one of the toughest gigs going. As mothers, we are socialized to ignore our own needs. Taking care of ourselves is considered selfish—we do for others first. But while we do for others, we also compare ourselves to other moms. You know the feeling—someone I know, let's call her Suzy, cooks a three-course dinner at home every night. Each meal is made from fresh, farm-to-table ingredients picked up daily at the local organic market. I, however, eat dinner out at least three times a week due to my long work hours, leaving my son to fend for himself (again). If I think about the disparity between Suzy and me, I begin to feel bad about myself because I am neither home to cook dinner nor can I keep up with Suzy's high standards when I am at home. Now, my inner competitiveness and drive begin to surface, and I have the urge to outdo Suzy with the next meal I cook.

Sound familiar?

There are many ways you can practice compassion and positively impact another person's day (and improve your own) using skills like consideration for others, kindness, empathy and understanding. Here are four examples:

Have considerate perspective. Don't get too caught up in your own world—take the time to anticipate and meet the needs of others. When speaking with someone, listen fully without judgment, and give them your full attention (no texting, no phone calls, no vacant staring!). Use direct eye contact. My father taught me to treat a custodian the same way as I would treat a CEO. I think about this most days, so I don't forget to thank the cleaning woman at the gym for her service or to leave a tip for the housekeeper at my hotel, who worked to ensure that I had a clean room. Not only do I believe that my efforts improve their day, but they definitely enhance mine.

Practice acts of kindness. Go out of your way to be kind to others. Help friends or family by offering to help with housework, run errands, cook a meal, etc. Let a coworker know you appreciate her. And, don't forget to say, "thank you" to your boss for his help—you'll both feel better. I frequent my local Starbucks near daily. Once or twice a month, I tell the Barista that I want to pay for the drink of the person behind me in line. I started doing this to see how I felt practicing random acts of kindness. Well, I found that this small offering liberated me (at least briefly) from any sense of myself as selfish, and helped to surface my more open and loving nature by giving to another without expectation. I felt very powerful with these acts of generosity, since they were unconditional and unattached. So, my "coffee offerings" have now become a welcome habit that I plan to sustain.

Show empathy. Compassion arises through empathy. Empathy is showing that you understand another's feelings or emotions, that you identify with the situation and care enough to place yourself in their shoes. I have found that validating another person's perspective and acknowledging them by not interrupting and by simply stating, "I understand" or "I can see" are great ways to communicate empathy.

Express yourself by sending a meaningful message. Send your compassionate feelings via a simple text message, email, or, better, handwritten letter or card to someone you care about. Just tell them you were thinking of them and that you love them. It is a simple way to show that they matter to you. I do this regularly with my son, who lives about twelve hundred miles away from me. It helps to keep us closely connected.

Here's reality. My own attitude and competitive nature were doing me in. I was negatively influenced by a set of arbitrary standards I set for myself. Who really cares whether I cook as well as Suzy except me? So I stopped comparing myself to Suzy. I started looking at myself rather than others, began charting a pathway to live just a little bit better each day by taking care of myself and putting my own needs first so I can better serve others. And let's face it: my son would rather eat frozen pizza than dover sole meunière—one of my favorites!

It's important to note that compassion isn't the same practice everywhere. An Eastern (or Buddhist) view is that we are all essentially compassionate by nature. The Dalai Lama sums it up succinctly: "Every human being has the same potential for compassion; the only question is whether we really take any care of that potential, and develop and implement it in our daily life." Buddhist compassion is directed toward all sentient beings and arises from the knowledge and wisdom of common suffering. The Western view of compassion is that it is a spontaneous feeling, directed toward an individual and arising from concern for another individual's suffering.

While Eastern and Western societies interpret compassion differently, there are important commonalities we can use in our leadership practice, such as respect and caring, empathy, giving selflessly and unconditionally, committed action, and offering a benefit to others without thought of gain.

Satya

On August 5, 2016, as the opening ceremony for the thirty-first Olympic Games kicked off in Rio de Janeiro, 207 nations joined to celebrate this pinnacle of sportsmanship, dedication, and talent. More than ten thousand athletes gathered to bring their unique stories of personal trial and overcoming odds to live their passion.

On August 15, 2016, US Olympic Swimmer and silver medalist Ryan Lochte said that he and James Feigen, Jack Conger, and Gunnar Bentz were robbed at a gas station in the early morning hours as they returned from a party.

The incident, however, was captured on closed-circuit television. Brazilian authorities said the American swimmers actually vandalized a gas station and then got into an altercation with security guards there.

After taking a public pounding for reporting a robbery story that police said was fabricated, Lochte apologized for "not being more careful and candid" in his description. He indicated that it was his fault that a fabricated story about a robbery caused an international Olympics scandal. Lochte said that he did not ask his teammates to corroborate his story and apologized "110 percent" to "the gas station owner, to Brazilian police, to the people of Rio and Brazil, everyone that came together to put on these wonderful games."

Lochte's shifting account of the incident and the resulting fallout stole the spotlight away, at least briefly, from an Olympic Games that the International Olympic Committee president declared "iconic." His four commercial sponsors dropped the twelve-time Olympic medal winner in response to the incident.

Athletic training and sports have played a big role in my personal development and my development as a leader. I recognize that business leaders and athletes share similar qualities. They must know when to lead, know when to follow, know when to pass to their teammates, and know when to ask for help. In addition, both business leaders and athletes must build a culture of truth telling by creating an environment in which it's preferable to tell the truth, no matter what others may think.

But the concept of truth telling goes far beyond business leaders and athletes. So how important is it?

Satya is the Sanskrit word for truth. This principle is based on the understanding that honest communication and action form the foundation of healthy relationships and societies. To develop an engaging culture, we must consider what we say, how we say it, and in what way it could impact others.

Workers often think their leaders don't want to hear the truth. When leaders encourage speaking the truth, it helps to create an atmosphere that encourages truth telling. People are more apt to speak up

How to Practice Truth Telling at Work

Drop the three "Fs"—facts, fear, and force—and focus on being empathetic to and considering employees' perspectives.

Validate another person's point of view. Validation is recognizing and acknowledging another person's point of view. Once you understand why another person believes what he believes, it's important to acknowledge it. Remember that acknowledgement does not necessarily mean agreement.

Encourage conversations that matter. People want to contribute but often can't see how. They experience most meetings as a waste of time. Give people permission to offer ideas and to express doubts.

Having conversations that matter at work can improve employee morale and increase employee loyalty. High-quality conversations lead to high-quality decisions and actions, which can translate into high-quality results.

Listen to what's really being said. Listening is a crucial skill for boosting another person's self-esteem. Listen to the entire message the other person is trying to communicate. Ask yourself: What is being said? What tone is being used? What is she doing with her body while speaking? What is she feeling?

Don't make bad news sound like good news—it's not. Get to the point, and make sure your message is clear and understood. Preparing a person or team for the information to come by saying, "I have something difficult that I need to tell you" is a good way to soften the blow.

about what's not working and to take the accountability and responsibility to do something about it when they do not fear attack or retribution.

Strategy consultant Brook Manville addressed the question head on in his *Forbes* article, "Is it OK for Leaders to Lie?" His conclusion was that we are trending toward a world in which we demand more honesty and transparency than we've come to expect from our leaders in both politics and business.

> Operating in this kind of world calls for a higher standard of transparency, and greater comfort with openness than earlier generations of leaders have known. In the new community context of networks, movements, and ecosystems, the ethical question now becomes a strategic competency of leaders: how can I tell the truth as often as humanly possible? But make no mistake. Most leaders will have to break new ground to find the more moral way.

The Edelman Trust Barometer for 2016, an online survey of over thirty-three thousand participants in twenty-eight countries, showed that peers and employees are more trusted than CEOs. While CEOs and senior leaders typically discuss the operational and financial aspects of a company when communicating, hearing information about personal values, experiences, and shared struggles that leaders have faced is more important to eight of ten employees. One out of every three employees does not trust his own company. So even "white lies"—lies meant to smooth discourse or deflect minor conflict—can lead to awkward situations and mistrust. For example, if a leader says, "I'm busy right now, but I'll call you later" to an employee—when he has no intention of calling her—such a brief and seemingly inconsequential statement can strain their relationship. Leaders must earn their constituents' trust and loyalty.

There are circumstances in which leaders often try to shield employees from the truth; this is a common occurrence when a company undergoes a merger or acquisition. Have you ever been through this type of situation? Your manager may say, "Not much will change, and your job is safe." Then, a few months later, radical changes and massive layoffs take everyone by surprise. Of course, this is not always the case, but you get the idea.

Truth telling matters. Truth leads to trust. It's not okay for leaders to lie.

Asteya

If the Sanskrit word *steya* means to steal, then *asteya* is the opposite—take nothing that does not belong to us. Asteya also means that if we are in a situation where someone entrusts something to us or confides in us, we do not take advantage of him or her. Nonstealing includes not only not taking what belongs to another without permission but also not using something for a different purpose other than for what it is intended or beyond the time permitted by its owner. The practice of asteya implies not taking *anything* that has not been freely given, including fostering a consciousness of how we ask for others' time. Demanding another's attention when not freely given is, in effect, stealing.

As leaders, we don't steal, right? How about stealing someone else's idea? Have you ever stolen someone else's idea and claimed it as yours? How about "fudging the numbers" to make your performance look better? Asteya means we should be mindful of accepting praise or credit we haven't earned. When we accept compliments for something that wasn't truly our doing, we are basically stealing from the person responsible.

Practicing the Yamas

It's easy to get caught up in the frenetic pace of the workday and the need to provide solutions *fast*—regardless of their efficacy. Here is a simple exercise you can perform in ten seconds or less to help you implement the lessons of the yamas in order to deliver a more mindful, compassionate, truthful, and powerful response. I started employing this exercise, The Pause, after my first visit to Japan.

Prior to speaking take a breath, *pause*, and ask yourself:

- Is it true?

- Is it necessary?

- Is it timely?

- Is it helpful?

- Can it be said with compassion?

I love the Japanese culture, which is based upon mutual respect and trust. The Japanese believe it is essential to show interest in your conversation while you are speaking, and thus they use intentional pauses with associated body language that generally includes a slight bow to indicate their respect. (I personally don't bow unless I am with a Japanese colleague.) In addition to showing respect, building trust through conversations is very important in Japanese society. Taking even just a few seconds to pause and think before you speak is a critical moment in building a stronger, more effective style of leadership.

It can be difficult to think of changing behaviors when the focus is on what *not* to do. How, then, can we cultivate nonstealing? One way is to frequently ask ourselves: Am I being mindful of what I am taking in this situation, both literally and metaphorically? Am I paying equal attention to what I am contributing and to the needs of those around me?

Saint Rocco Catholic Elementary School in Johnston, Rhode Island, has students keep a daily Good Deeds Journal. The school stresses the need for children to feel confident and have a positive self-image. At the start of each day students write in their journal a good deed they performed the day before in school, at home, or in the community. Students learn that a good deed can be anything that contributes to another person's happiness. In this way the journal helps to prevent peer cruelty and serves as a reminder of what the students are contributing rather than what they are taking in everyday life. Could we experience a societal transformation if everyone kept a daily Good Deeds Journal?

Thou Shalt Not Steal

Character is the combination of personality traits, values, and virtues. Character is a central, key element of leadership.

- Leaders own their choices and actions.

- Leaders don't blame others for their decisions.

- Leaders recognize that their decisions impact others.

- Leaders don't take credit for other people's work.

- Wise leaders create shared contexts for employees to learn from one another.

Brahmacharya

In our culture success is often associated with money and power. Wielding power is an important yet highly delicate aspect of leadership. In the worst cases power can be abused or avoided, and in the best cases it can be used judiciously and for worthy goals.

In the Western world the word *brahmacharya* has often been interpreted literally as celibacy, but it actually means "living in divine consciousness." *Brahma* literally means the "divine consciousness" and *charya*, in this context, means "living" or "one who is established in." That may sound lofty and perhaps unattainable, but it simply means control of the senses or living in moderation. Brahmacharya means having control over our impulses of excess. As a society we continually strive for *more* in our lives. Our Western culture is materialistic and consumerist. When I practice brahmacharya I do so from a perception of moderation and control over my impulses of excess, whether that's in shopping, dining out, travel—really anything. I limit my indulgences. Well, most of the time.

We're constantly waiting for our lives to be complete with *more* and striving for a day that will never come. Because we are in a state of deferred living—what we have now is not enough—we miss living in the moment.

A few years ago I wanted to take a bike trip to Ireland. I looked through lots of outdoors journals and trips guides and saw that the countryside was beautiful and the landscape serene. I was excited to see green hills and quaint villages and to immerse myself in the Irish culture for a week. After discussion with my partner, however, we decided that the trip was too costly that year and that we would go instead on a bicycle trip through southern Vermont. Well, we had been to Vermont several times, and I found myself lacking enthusiasm prior to and during the trip. Here's the problem: I failed to fully appreciate the Vermont countryside—Vermont also has green hills, quaint villages, and a unique culture. By wishing I was in Ireland, I missed the full experience of Southern Vermont.

In the work world we often seek power or position. Leaders must understand the power they hold—the positive effects of using it properly and the ill effects when used negatively. Those who use their power appropriately can motivate staff, inspire loyalty and commitment, and push employees to aspire to greater achievement. In contrast, those who abuse their power bring down morale, create turnover, incur grievances, and cost the company money in lost productivity. A third dynamic—leaders who avoid the use of the power they are entrusted with—can create confusion, anxiety, and a sense of helplessness in staff.

Leaders are most effective when they understand they are in positions of authority—and they influence, inspire, and mentor their way to success. In a broader sense leaders may balance this power dynamic by fostering wide-ranging organizational impact that extends to the community and connects to social causes. Some businesses are offering a percentage of their profits or matching purchases. Blake Mycoskie created Toms Shoes after witnessing the hardships faced by children growing up without shoes. Toms Shoes donates a pair of shoes to a child in need for every pair they sell. With their "One for One" campaign, Tom's has given away more than 60 million pairs of shoes and has now expanded into bags, eyewear, and coffee.

The "Buy One Give One" model is attractive to consumers and is consequently a potentially powerful method to bolster social change. There is power of the "one," as consumers understand that their purchase will benefit "a child in need"—a premise that encourages consumers to use the power of their dollars for the greater good. As seen in their bottom lines, these companies have taken advantage of the nature of people to exert great effort to rescue "the one" whose needy plight comes to their attention. Although critics have pointed out that sporadic influxes of goods will not address the issues underlying poverty or limited access to education and healthcare in developing nations, such efforts focus consumer awareness on the need for social change and a better balance of power and authority across all lines.

Toms' corporate culture is bound to its social mission. For example, once a month the company holds a "Happy Helping Hour" in which members of a charitable organization visit Toms to engage with employees in an activity, such as preparing care packages for women in domestic abuse shelters. Toms chooses employees who care about the company's social mission and will work hard to integrate sustainable and responsible practices into all they do.

Aparigraha

I often find myself holding on to the notion of a right or wrong way of doing things—clearly the right way is the one I'm choosing! Despite my best efforts to maintain a yogic mindset, I continually fight against my type A tendencies, which include a sense of time and urgency for any given task, a need to "do it right the first time," and a quest for "the best" outcome.

Aparigraha means to take only what is necessary and not to take advantage of a situation or act greedy. Aparigraha also implies nonpossessiveness, or letting go of our attachments to things as well as our need to control people or our surroundings. Nonaccumulating simply means confidence in our existence and abilities and knowledge of ourselves.

Preventing Burnout

There are things you can do whenever you're stressed to keep yourself mentally and physically healthy and to avoid reaching the point of burnout.

Slow down and take a break.

Take regular time out for yourself each day to relax and unwind.

Set aside at least one hour each day to "switch off" from technology.

Establish boundaries so you reduce how often you overextend yourself.

Reevaluate your goals and priorities so you include activities in your daily routine that support your happiness.

Ask for help—we all need it.

Reach out to supportive people in your life to talk and to receive support.

Don't compare. Theodore Roosevelt said, "Comparison is the thief of Joy." It's simple and true.

Be grateful. Gratitude is an affirmation of goodness. It leads to forgiveness and paying it forward. Practicing gratitude is a reliable means to increase happiness.

Aparigraha is one of the central teachings in the ancient yogic text *The Bhagavad Gita,* which consists of seven hundred verses and is mainly a conversation between Krishna and Arjuna taking place on the battlefield of Kurukshetra just prior to the start of a climactic war. Krishna, a major Hindu deity, counsels Arjuna, a fine archer and peerless warrior. Krishna begins with the tenet that the soul is both eternal and immortal. Any "death" on the battlefield would involve only the shedding of the body, but the soul is permanent. Krishna goes on to expound on the yogic paths of devotion, action, meditation, and knowledge. He states, "Let your concern be with action alone, and never with the fruits of action. Do not let the results of action be your motive, and do not be attached to inaction." Krishna is essentially saying that we should never concern ourselves with the outcome of a situation; we should only concern ourselves with what we're actually doing right now.

Fear of not being enough often drives our desire for possession or attachment. How often do we worry so much about what might come of the effort we put into a project at work that we never really enjoy the work itself? Can we stop being concerned with what *could* happen and instead enjoy what *is* happening? So often we worry whether we'll be successful enough or good enough that we forget why we started a project in the first place. When we know we are enough, just as we are, we can let go of that which doesn't serve us. Aparigraha offers us freedom—the freedom to work and do what we love without worrying about the outcome, to rely less on material possessions to bring us happiness, and to experience all that life has to offer.

Understanding Aparigraha

Our lives, our heads, and our schedules are filled with "stuff." Generally too much stuff. The concept of aparigraha refers to nonpossessiveness—not being possessive of material items, ideas, people, or places. Practicing aparigraha does not require that we get rid of all our things but rather that we get rid of our *attachments* to those things. By releasing attachments and letting go of what is no longer useful, we experience more freedom and become open to new ideas, relationships, and ways of being. Ask yourself: What am I holding on to or clinging to in my life? Does this serve me? Should I let it go?

Tips for Practicing Aparigraha

Get rid of what you don't need. Possessions take up space and energy, so getting rid of unneeded items can be a liberating experience that creates both physical and mental space. There are three hundred thousand items in the average American home. So consider giving things away that you think you "might use" but in reality have not used in years. When you let go of things from the past, you become able to live more fully in the present.

Forgive others and yourself. Free, nurture, and heal yourself by offering forgiveness to those who have hurt you as well as to yourself. Letting go of painful memories from the past is a key step toward leading a fulfilling and empowered life. Who wants to live with anger and resentment?

Be generous. We live in a culture often characterized by fear. Generosity is the opposite of fear. Giving without expecting anything in return is an act of generosity. So share your time, your energy, and your expertise generously with others.

Reach out to family and friends randomly to let them know you are thinking of them and are sending them love. How do *you* feel?

Have a positive attitude. Clinging to negative thoughts and emotions can become a vicious cycle. Negative thoughts reinforce negative emotions, which in turn lead to negative actions. By replacing negative thoughts with positive thinking, we develop a more optimistic attitude that leads to new opportunities for joy and harmony in our lives.

As leaders we must become nimble at working with fluctuating priorities, high expectations, and in complex environments with ongoing conflict and ambiguity. We must focus on the future, toward innovation, development, and sustainable corporate growth. The present is often viewed as nothing more than a platform for the envisioning of and positioning for the future.

The five yamas, like yoga, are all encompassing and welcoming to everyone. As we develop these "wise characteristics" we build a foundation for our own health and happiness. So I challenge you to stay in the present long enough to commit to a process of sustainable personal growth. The practices and exercises I've outlined in these pages will help you understand and implement the yamas and other yogic principles, even if you never attempt a yoga pose. In fact, my goal is not to convert you into a yoga-pants-wearing devotee (unless you really enjoy it—and I hope that you will, as yoga is one of the few physical practices that is adaptable to nearly everybody).

I've made a strong commitment to my own corporate career and believe the answer to better leadership is not to opt out and choose an alternative path but rather to allow these transformative yogic principles to inspire and enable me to grow and achieve more than I ever thought I could in my chosen profession. And yoga has helped me achieve better work-life balance so I don't sacrifice the people and things important to me beyond work. How? Yoga is about balance— mental, physical, and spiritual. Through my practice I am more

Practical Application of the Yamas: Observation

Most everything is relational. How are you doing with your relationships?

Observe your relationship to the five yamas of:

Nonviolence

Truthfulness

Nonstealing

Nonexcess

Nonpossessiveness

Does restraining yourself come easily? Probably not.

By observing our behavior we strengthen our powers of awareness, will, and discernment. We fortify our character and improve our relationships.

self-aware, discerning, and honest with myself. I am more available to others. And I am better able to appreciate the moment and live in the present (most of the time).

What about you? Practicing the yamas will help you to develop a secure foundation upon which you can achieve more confidence, strength, resilience, and balance. Sound good? Let's proceed.

Self-Reflection

1. What are your core values? How do you manifest them in your life?

2. Do your thoughts, words, and actions come from a place of love and compassion?

3. Do you speak your truth, or are you scared and worried that you might hurt others' feelings? How can you balance your truths and your fears to practice satya (truth) and ahimsa (compassion)?

4. Do you want and crave what others have, or are you happy as you are?

5. Is your life in balance? Do you live with moderation?

6. Is your life cluttered? Are you holding on to lots of extra things, or do you live with simplicity?

7. Do you practice forgiveness? For yourself? For others?

2

Embracing Rigorous Self-Improvement

"In reading the lives of great men, I found that the
first victory they won was over themselves . . .
self-discipline with all of them came first."
—US President Harry S. Truman (1884–1972)

In its simplest sense, self-improvement starts with basic self-care.

Part of self-care involves caring for your own environment and keeping a neat desk or workspace. I'll be the first to tell you that this deceptively simple practice is one of the hardest to commit to! I seem to be forever cleaning and straightening up my home and office, but no matter how hard I try, my office is always a mess. I usually have multiple projects going at once, and there are stacks of papers and files on my desk, computer table, the top of my bookcase, and, at times, even on the floor. My excuse is that I'm too busy to clean up the clutter. Of course, I claim to know where everything is, but I'm often at a loss to find things (the title of the new car I bought over a year ago—I know it's here somewhere!). A disorganized space can lead to feeling anxious and unprepared, not beneficial to a productive workday, much less effective leadership.

Periodically I get the urge to clean and organize my office. If I can't find anything in my office, how can I be productive at work, much less function as an effective leader? However, I typically quit about halfway into the process, as the task is simply too daunting. Once I even hired a professional organizer. We worked together for about eight hours, and *voilà*—everything was clean and organized at last!—well, for about a week, and then the piles began creeping up again. Ugh. Sound familiar?

In a more recent attempt to banish clutter forever, I read Marie Kondo's blockbuster best-sellers, *The Life Changing Magic of Tidying Up* and *Spark Joy*. Kondo recommends asking yourself whether an item "sparks joy" before deciding to keep it or, if not, thank it for its service and toss it. So I asked myself if each pencil and piece of paper on my desk sparked joy—but when the answer was no, I was still afraid to toss them for fear that I might need them at a later time. I didn't realistically expect to have a joyful relationship with each item on my desk! However, being a Kondo fan, I kept on believing her method would lead to a better way. I took a slightly different approach and made priorities by asking what was really important to me in the moment: cleaning clutter or pursuing a project; cleaning clutter or meeting a friend, cleaning clutter or going to a movie. In addition, I began to treat the things in my office with more respect and became more inclined to find a "home" for each item I did not purge. So although I have not found a tidiness nirvana, the Kondo method is supporting me in *slowly* creating better office order.

Bottom line: know yourself. It's great to be inspired or take advice from others, but real change is a matter of individual preferences and readiness. And it's about a continuous commitment. I'm realistic—no eight-hour organizing session is going to suddenly change my ingrained habit—but I recognize there's always a way to improve.

In this chapter we'll explore the *niyamas*, or individual practices that can help us build our personal and professional development. The second of the eight limbs of yoga, niyama, a Sanskrit term, literally means positive duties or observances. Where the yamas are universally applicable moral precepts, the niyamas are focused practices for the individual. They require us to stop and think about how our own personal growth and balance can be improved, and ask us to dedicate time and effort toward changing our approach and putting a plan into place. But the reward is worth the effort, and anyone can create powerful positive change using these simple steps.

We'll now look closely at five main practices, or niyamas: cleanliness (*saucha*), contentment (*santosha*), self-restraint (*tapas*), self-study (*svadhyaya*), and devotion *(Ishvara Pranidhana)*. Together these niyamas describe how we should act toward ourselves and encourage us to live and work better by applying a little discipline to areas we may not always pay attention to. They suggest that while we seek to attain mastery, we must also relinquish control. What does this mean?

Well, take my messy office—my "solution" of hiring a personal organizer may have worked temporarily, but because it wasn't my own system, it didn't work long term. I wasn't really engaged in the process, so I had no ownership over it. Thus, even though she showed me exactly what to do, the personal organizer couldn't prevent the piles from creeping up again once we parted ways. Similarly, even the motivating work of Marie Kondo did not get me to quickly change my habits. While I initially beat myself up for not being able to master the KonMari method, which I assumed was the "right way," I realized that the "right way" is whatever works for me, not what works for Marie Kondo. A revelation, to say the least!

So I admit I haven't been able to keep my office as neat as I would like to, but I've finally figured out a way to organize things as best I

The Niyamas:
Self-Improvement in Five Practices

- **Saucha**—cleanliness

- **Santosha**—contentment

- **Tapas**—self-restraint

- **Svadhyaya**—self-study

- **Ishvara Pranidhana**—devotion

can. And I continue this work, determined. I've internalized the need to maintain self-discipline, and I let go of the need to control every messy pile because it's a system I've chosen myself, and it works for me.

Everyone struggles with some element they'd like to improve but must work to maintain discipline. Many people make resolutions every New Year to get in shape and start exercising regularly. However, over a third of resolutions don't make it past January, and over three-quarters are abandoned soon after. These resolutions typically don't work. Why? Well, it's in large part because they represent what you *think* you *should* be doing rather than what you really *want* to be doing. We cannot make viable decisions based on other people's expectations. So forget what you and others think you ought to be doing, and figure out what you want and what's important to you. For example, although my office is still somewhat disorganized, my body is in excellent condition. I'm very proud of my lifelong dedication to physical fitness. I am over fifty, but I have competed—and held my own—against women in their thirties! I am certainly far from a professional athlete, but fitness is something I love and enjoy, and I've made sufficient time to train because it's a genuine part of who I am. Fitness is not something I force myself to do—well, most of the time.

In the beginning it's easy to hate any regimen, especially if you don't see results right away. Motivation and commitment are hard to come by when your goal seems impossible—and maybe that's the problem. A second problem is that as soon as you set yourself a goal, you're saying to yourself that you want more in your life than you have right now. The very nature of goals is that they make you look forward to what's next, never appreciating what you have right now. Goals may lead you to you feel "less than" because they represent something you don't have now but you aspire to have sometime in the future. There is real value in accepting where things are in the present as well as enjoying the experience of creating opportunities for the future.

If you're constantly trying to lose an unrealistic amount of weight or run a marathon when you've never finished a 5K, you'll only get trapped in a frustrating cycle of despair. What if, instead, you made healthy eating habits and movement a more natural part of your daily life and committed internally to making these things a true part of you? Maybe you decide to eat a more balanced diet and stop beating yourself up for indulging in sweets or fried foods every once in a while. Maybe you start taking walks in nature or jogging with your dog instead of dragging yourself to the gym or out on the high school track. The real value of self-improvement is when it happens organically, not as a forced punishment. Only when we balance the need for control and letting go can we achieve a true sense of change from within.

Think of one area of your life you have tried to improve without success. If you are waiting for a miracle or for the stars to align in your favor to get moving, STOP NOW. That perfect moment will never come.

Six Steps to Make a Meaningful, Lasting Change in Your Life:

1. Assess your current situation and identify the change you need to make.

   My office is a mess and this is frustrating me and slowing down my progress.

2. Develop a mindset toward improvement and outline a clear goal.

   I will rid myself of the clutter in my office.

3. Commit to a plan of action, define exactly what you want and how you are going to get there, and develop a timeline to reach your goal.

   I will begin today to evaluate and to either put away or discard ten items per day in my office. There are about one hundred items that are not in order, so I will complete my goal in ten days. I envision my neat and inviting space!

4. Focus on what is truly important to achieve your goal.

   I will spend half my time creating a system for organization and half my time cleaning and organizing.

5. Take responsibility, and hold yourself accountable.

   I write down my goal (no office clutter!) and use a Goals Journal—I like the SmartLife PUSH Journal—to keep track of my most important tasks on a daily basis. I allocate time each day for these tasks. I advise my family members about my plan and ask them to check in with me daily to help me stay committed.

6. Celebrate your success!

   I pause to enjoy what I have accomplished and suggest that you do so too. In the words of Oprah Winfrey, "The more you praise and celebrate your life, the more there is in life to celebrate."

Saucha

Saucha, translated as "purification, cleanliness," is a clearing out on all levels. Saucha means cleanliness of body, mind, spirit, and surroundings. Practicing saucha leads us toward a pure and positive life. Saucha refers to what we in the West call self-care: developing good habits to keep our minds and bodies in good condition, from a healthy diet, physical cleanliness, and purity of our environment to a healthy attitude toward our family, coworkers, and friends. Observing saucha is both a practice and a never-ending quest.

If this concept is new to you, these ideas may sound a bit "off the wall." What does saucha mean *exactly*? Outer body? Inner mind? Cluttered office?

Let's again consider my messy desk. Saucha in action is, in part, my recognition that everything has its place and there is a place for everything. However, while I have evolved in many ways in my efforts at purification in both my mind and body, I remain far from perfect in terms of organizing my desk. Because I practice saucha in many other areas of my life, I've often wondered: Why I can't get my act together, and is my messy desk really *that* bad? Those notorious for their messy desks include US president Donald Trump; creator of modern computing, Alan Turing; and theoretical physicist Albert Einstein. Einstein is quoted as saying, "If a cluttered desk is a sign of a cluttered mind, of what, then, is an empty desk a sign?"

Organizing expert Peter Walsh states, "If you have a cluttered office, you risk being seen as inefficient or not on top of your work. Disorganization suggests a degree of incompetence that clouds your abilities. You run the risk of jeopardizing your chance of a promotion." But in contrast researchers at the University of Minnesota's Carlson School of Management reported that while working at a clean desk

Everyday Saucha

To integrate saucha into your everyday life and work ask yourself these five questions:

1. Do I strive to keep my body, clothing, food, home, and work environment clean?

2. Am I breathing freely and effortlessly? (The breath helps to cleanse us of toxins that have built up in the body and mind).

3. Am I eating high-quality, unrefined, and minimally processed foods such as vegetables and fruits, whole grains, healthy fats, and good sources of protein?

4. Am I keeping my life clean and pure? Is my purpose pure? Are my motives unselfish? Do I wear a "mask" to adapt to different people and situations?

5. Am I comfortable with myself? Can I just "be myself" without pretense? Am I comfortable spending time in solitude?

may promote healthy eating, generosity, and conventionality, working at a messy desk may spark creative thinking and new ideas. (News flash: I have always considered myself very creative, so, of course, my desk is messy!) Disorderly environments seem to inspire creativity and breaking free from the status quo, while orderly environments imply conventional attitudes and thinking.

Now, I'm confident—or, at least I hope—that people see me as competent, even if my desk is piled with papers, but I do believe an organized workspace helps me minimize distractions and increases my productivity (even if that means simply finding an important document quickly, without wasting time sifting through the piles!). But in the spirit of relinquishing control, I don't let myself get held back by the mess either—I greatly value my ability to think freely and creatively, and if I am onto something that feels innovative, the need to clear the clutter takes a backseat. By practicing saucha in my workspace I trust that my efforts to clear my desk will let my mind remain active and open.

Try This in Two Minutes
Begin to Address Clutter

Is your stuff controlling your life? Go one item at a time. Getting started with decluttering means picking up one object and taking it one object at a time.

Step into a cluttered room at home.

Pick up an object and ask yourself:

> Do I honestly need this item?
>
> Does it have significance in my life?
>
> Does it serve a purpose?
>
> Do I use it?
>
> Do I love it?

If the answer to all these questions is no, then get rid of it now, before reading on.

Repeat this exercise daily—you are practicing saucha.

Does Our Attire Reflect
Who We Are at Work?

When I think of leaders who embody focus and presence, US senator Cory Booker and retired four-star general Colin Powell come to mind—both are elegant, poised, and speak with confidence and authority. They also just look the part.

Although I don't work in government nor do I wear a military uniform, I prefer to dress for work on the more formal side myself and feel comfortable in business attire. (I joke that I *prefer* working at a more formal headquarters in New York City over casual offices in other areas because I feel more at home wearing dresses and suits!) That's me—you may feel totally differently.

These days many corporate cultures have eschewed business attire for a much more casual look and presence. Steve Jobs and Mark Zuckerberg have inspired a generation of T-shirt-and-jeans-wearing employees and CEOs who may look loose but are in fact extremely serious about their work and leadership style. When Mr. Zuckerberg was asked why he wears the same gray T-shirt every day, he stated, "I really want to clear my life so that I have to make as few decisions as possible about anything except how to best serve this community." The point is that your attitude and behavior transcends your clothes—even when I wore scrubs in the hospital as a medical resident and fellow, I commanded respect because I demonstrated authority and authenticity. *That's* what people respond to, not an expensive suit or the hipster hoodie. My advice is to find the work "uniform" that feels comfortable for you—and then spend your time and energy focusing on the task at hand. Let your poise and posture speak volumes and allow your look to follow as an extension of these attributes.

Santosha

Contentment is being satisfied with what you have and who you are—in the present moment. In the Western world most of us have been taught to believe that contentment is linked to our accomplishments or constantly getting more. Our basic value is that "more is better," and we place a variety of personal qualifications on our contentment. We think, "I'll be happy when I get married," or "I'll be content when I get a promotion" or " . . . when I buy a luxury car" or " . . . when I run a marathon." You get the idea: we feel like we can never be content until we attain that next level—we are always striving for change, improvement, or the next promotion, but the truth is that we can create it now. Santosha is to be content, to just be. It's important to be clear on this: contentment does not preclude ambition. It does not mean that you will not want more. Contentment is gratitude, appreciation, and acceptance *for the way things are now.*

I used to find myself always wanting more and, admittedly, jealous of the successes of others. Following a pediatrics residency and pediatric oncology fellowship I started my formal career in academic medicine, working as a faculty member at a major university. While I maintained my academic mindset, I realized about five years into this position that I wanted more global reach and to develop entrepreneurial skills (marketing, management, finance, and negotiation) more than I had initially realized. I decided to transition to an industry career and was hired into a research and development position at a large pharmaceutical company. All good? No, not in my mind anyway. Why? Because I essentially had to start over. I was at a low rank—at least I perceived it to be low—and could not happily internalize such an assignment. I wanted to be a leader—at the time I felt that I had somehow been demoted, but it was my own doing! Slowly but surely I worked my way up by confidently meeting my goals and deliverables and by taking the initiative to do more than required. I learned all aspects of bringing a new product to market and began to excel at translating science from bench to product to customer. When I allowed myself the opportunity to grow more organically rather than pushing toward that next higher-ranking position, my organizational aptitude, skills, and positioning improved.

Through my yoga practice I have now internalized that the happiness gained through success or materialism is only temporary. I realize that every person whom I momentarily think has everything—doesn't. Contentment is a deep-seated sense of accepting—and fully experiencing—where you are at any given moment. Too often we get so busy that we don't even notice where we are, and when we finally come up

Try This in Two Minutes

Finding Contentment

Take a few moments to look around your office (or wherever you might be reading this book). Describe your space without making any judgments. Instead of saying the room is cheerful or dreary (words of judgment), simply observe the texture of the carpet or floor, the color of the room, and the positioning of your furniture. Perhaps the walls are beige, the desk is facing the window, the fabric on your chair is slightly worn, and there is a photo of someone you love next to your computer. By noticing without judging, we allow ourselves to be aware of the present moment. Contentment comes when we are most aware of the present moment, and through the power of contentment, happiness becomes a more viable choice.

for air we focus on where we were or where we want to be. Does this feel familiar? Before we can be content with where we are, we must first be *aware* of where we are. The yogic premise is that what exists in the present moment is enough. Contentment is also about being happy with who you are. Many people who have reached a certain level of success don't find contentment. Why? They are always driven to want more and are unhappy with themselves. I did not find contentment by having a "successful" career; I found it by trusting myself and letting go of my tendency to compare myself to others or to ideals I could never achieve. Living with greater contentment has freed me from the unnecessary suffering of always wanting things to be different, and I now have gratitude and appreciation for my life just as it is.

How often do you just take a moment to notice and accept it?

Tapas

The word *tapas* is derived from the Sanskrit verb "tap," which means to burn. Tapas has traditionally been interpreted to mean "fiery discipline," and we use it to focus our energy, create fervor, and increase strength and confidence. Self-discipline is your ability to control your desires, emotions, impulses, and behaviors to stay focused on what needs to get done to successfully meet your goals. It is a key attribute of good leaders. Such individuals have a sense of inner calm and outer resolve. They are well organized in that they have clear objectives and priorities— whether or not their offices are cluttered—and they demonstrate willpower and determination in everything they do. This level of self-control allows them to persist in the face of difficulties and to exert a more positive, powerful influence on others.

My father had a military background, and thus his leadership style was based on the concepts of duty, service, and self-sacrifice. He always

Tips on Cultivating Contentment

1. **Pause.** When you find yourself unhappy with someone or trying to change them, pause. Take a deep breath, and remind yourself to accept them as they are and to identify and embrace their good qualities.

2. **Stop buying stuff you don't need.** When you feel the urge to buy something think about whether it's a *need* or a *want*. If the item is a *want* think about why you are not content with what you have now. As yourself: Do I *need* to buy this now? Wait a few days—yes, the wait can be like torture!—and see if the urge to buy it dissipates prior to your final decision. Perhaps you will let it go.

3. **Show people you appreciate them.** Be present. Offer kind words and actions to help build up your emotional bank account.

4. **Practice gratitude.** Each day identify at least one person, pet, or thing that enriches your life. When you find yourself unhappy with something or with what you don't have, take a moment to experience gratitude for all the good things in your life.

5. **Learn to enjoy simple things that don't cost money.** Good conversations. Walking in nature. Reading a good book. A trip to the beach.

6. **Live in the moment.** Don't postpone happiness by waiting for a day when your life is less busy, less stressful, or "things will change for the better." That day may never come. Instead, look for opportunities to savor the small pleasures of daily life. Focus on the positives *today* rather than dwelling on the past or worrying about the future.

put his family first and saved money for many years in order to allow me to complete college and medical school with limited debt. He was also a high school principal who powerfully influenced students and colleagues alike by putting them first. So I grew up appreciating and understanding the value of self-discipline and self-sacrifice. I have come to recognize that in large part self-discipline has allowed me to stay the course in achieving my goals and dreams.

On a more personal, inner level, self-discipline means you act with the same leadership qualities that you consider desirable and necessary in public even when you are alone. It is easy to attempt to deceive yourself when you're alone and assume no one is watching. A true leader exercises self-discipline in her thoughts and actions, even when she believes no one can see her.

Many people feel they lack self-discipline in certain areas and often chalk it up to, "Well, that's just the way I am." We all must work within the parameters of our natural personalities, but self-discipline is essential for strong leadership: without it, you lose credibility. Think about it. August 8, 1974, Richard M. Nixon became the first American president to resign from office during impeachment proceedings and in the midst of the Watergate affair. In a farewell speech delivered from the Oval office he said, "By taking this action, I hope that I will have hastened the start of the process of healing which is so desperately needed in America." On April 10, 2017, Robert Bentley, Alabama governor, resigned amid a sex scandal and series of criminal investigations. These individuals clearly lacked self-discipline. True self-discipline allows you to lead by example and go the extra mile for your company and employees.

I have struggled over the years to see myself as a leader. Using the principles of self-discipline and self-awareness—which I'll elaborate on in the next chapter—I've been able to work hard on my self-development. Most leaders did not arrive there already formed; their success is a direct result of their determination to press forward through difficulties, resistance, and setbacks. Cultivating self-discipline enhances their level of confidence through a greater sense of control. They get more done in less time.

We can all practice the self-discipline needed to become great leaders. Think about the areas you feel passionate enough to make improvements—a strong desire can help you get started and stick to the changes you set out to make. Then you can tackle areas you aren't as sure you can succeed. Once you start to see the positive growth you've created with smaller goals, you'll be surprised how quickly you'll take on more difficult ones.

Soon you'll experience the greatest reward of all: to succeed as a leader with integrity, compassion, and a job well done.

A mentor, someone whom you trust and is typically a more senior-ranking individual at work, allows you to share your wins and seek feedback on challenging issues so you gain experiential advice. My mentor, Liz, heard me speak during several important teleconferences. She mentioned that I constantly referred to "the leadership" when I spoke and what we as a team had to do to challenge or support them. What's wrong with that? Well, the truth was that I was actually part of the leadership team. By excluding myself from the group in my discussions I came across as a victim. Liz asked whether I felt like a leader, and my honest response at the time was "not really." Thank goodness our conversations were confidential—what if anyone else knew my response? In many ways I thought I still needed to achieve the most senior organizational rank to *really* be a leader.

I gave the situation and her feedback some thought, as her opinion was always worth listening to and considering. My attitude was actually sabotaging my career and limiting my opportunity for

Challenge Yourself

How many times have you told yourself you were going to make a change but didn't follow through? Challenge yourself by identifying *one* thing you can do this month to enhance your self-discipline, and give yourself one week to outline how you will accomplish your goal. Then go for it! Don't make excuses! At the heart of any successful person is self-discipline. Whether in terms of your diet, fitness, work ethic, or relationships, self-discipline is the number-one trait needed to accomplish goals, lead a healthy lifestyle, and, ultimately, be happy.

advancement—and I needed to change it. The quality of my leadership really mattered to me. Once I acknowledged the problem, I developed a plan to address it. I asked Liz and a few other colleagues to monitor how I spoke in subsequent meetings and to give me feedback. I wanted to know when my words and message came across with a victim mentality.

Hans Christian Andersen's fairytale "The Emperor's New Clothes" is not just a parable on the consequences of vanity; it has a secondary message that reinforces the sense of isolation many leaders feel: those around you are reluctant to offer direct feedback on your behavior. Unfortunately some may even choose to criticize you behind your back. This has happened to me, and it is certainly counterproductive—for everyone. Most people can recall with several traumatic episodes from their pasts where they have given or received negative feedback. These negative experiences can linger in our minds and become a source of ongoing upset and anxiety. We all have behavioral blind spots, and

Six Steps to Develop
Better Self-Discipline at Work

1. **Establish a clear vision and plan.** Develop and communicate your vision for the future and your plan to achieve it. Successful leaders communicate in such a way that others "own" the vision and seek to execute the plan.

2. **Set simple rules.** Set some conditions you will commit to upholding. Write them down and keep them visible so you are more likely to adhere to them. Adhering to a specific set of rules or standards will help you to shape and align your thoughts and behaviors effectively to the task at hand.

3. **Limit your list of goals.** If we try to achieve too many goals at once, we find ourselves distracted. Limiting our list of goals helps us increase our chances of success by focusing our energy on a short list instead of spreading ourselves too thin with the risk of not accomplishing much of anything.

4. **Measure your progress.** Keep a record of your progress so you can see whether you are making the desired progress or slipping behind and need to take corrective action.

5. **Hold yourself accountable.** Self-discipline involves consistently managing yourself and adjusting your behavior to adapt to changing conditions and circumstances. Invariably setbacks occur, but if you can identify the obstacles and keep your emotions in check as you work through them, you'll be able to refocus your efforts on the task at hand. As a leader, your behavior sets the tone for the rest of the group, so it's critical that you practice self-awareness and hold yourself accountable for your decisions and actions.

6. **Reward yourself.** By creating multiple small wins for yourself and your team as you move forward, you'll maintain a "feel good" factor that keeps up momentum and supports continued progress.

constructive feedback is very important for growth—we should never be afraid to ask for it directly. Feedback helps us to better understand ourselves. Without feedback, how can we understand why we do or don't win the deal, get the promotion, or are chosen for the team? Highly successful leaders typically ask for feedback often. Rather than being fearful of feedback, they are comfortable receiving information about their behavior from their bosses, their colleagues, and their subordinates. They then typically engage in self-reflection and introspection, both critical elements for behavioral change.

My plan was to focus my thoughts on my own leadership style and to change my behavior and take ownership of it so I demonstrated true leadership qualities. During discussions I started to listen better and tried to understand the position and perspective of the others involved in the conversation. I also worked to improve my own communication style when speaking directly with colleagues and supervisors and especially during teleconferences, when the element of body language is removed. Most importantly, I worked hard to truly believe and to internalize that I *was* a leader.

I still remind myself daily that I am a leader. I usually believe it.

Svadhyaya

One of the most important things a leader can do for themselves is to become more aware of what motivates them and their decision making.

Svadhyaya means to remember, contemplate, or meditate on the self. Svadhyaya is the practice of rigorous and honest self-inquiry and self-examination, which leads to greater self-awareness, critical for effective leadership. Greek philosopher Aristotle said, "Knowing yourself is the beginning of all wisdom."

In yoga we observe the responses of our body and the reactions of our mind as we move through our practice. As leaders we must study ourselves so we become more aware of who we really are beyond our personality, thoughts, emotions, and body. The self-evaluation leads us to a deeper connection with ourselves and a better understanding of our true essence—the greatest good within.

I know—more yoga-speak. But many successful leaders follow such practices. American business magnate Warren Buffett, for example, has made it a habit to write down the reasons he is making an investment decision and later look back to see what went right or wrong. Peter Drucker, in "Managing Oneself," wrote, "Whenever you make a decision or take a key decision, write down what you expect will happen. Nine or twelve months later, compare the results with what you expected." Drucker called this self-reflection process "feedback analysis" and said it was "the only way to discover your strengths." The key to the effectiveness of the feedback analysis is to better understand your rationale and motivations for decision making and to reflect and evaluate outcomes. I had to seriously assess my own leadership style as well as my strengths and areas needing improvement prior to making any changes.

We also need to have an accurate read on how others decode the messages we send. After meetings pause and ask yourself: How did I make others feel? How did others perceive me? On occasion you could even request feedback from small focus groups of people you trust and whose opinions you value. It's never a bad idea take a hard look in the mirror to learn and grow. A look in the mirror can be a time for honest introspection. If you could see that your actions did not produce the outcome you intended, you may be more inclined to change your behavior, especially if you envision a different, more positive outcome. Practicing emotional and social awareness will help you strengthen relationships and support your efforts to build a successful team or network.

Take Cues from Others

Make a list of the leaders you most admire, whether they are famous figures or those with whom you have a personal or professional connection. Across from each name list three to five characteristics that make each person a great leader. Now, circle the qualities that consistently appear and reflect on how you can grow and implement these qualities into your own life and leadership style. If you've listed someone you know personally, consider interviewing them to better understand how they developed these characteristics you so admire. You may be surprised at their response to your request and their answers to your questions. Believe it or not, most people are flattered to be interviewed. They are eager to share about themselves. A successful leadership path is generally a rigorous one. The interview process itself may help you better understand that person, strengthen your relationship, and feel more bonded to them.

Ishvara Pranidhana

Ishvara pranidhana—devotion or surrender to a higher source—is the fifth and final niyama and the most frequent statement in the Yoga sutras. This element is essential to yoga, leadership, and life. Very often *ishvara* is taken to mean "God," but it is really your personal approach to the divine. It's your choice to connect with whatever resonates personally with you. It may be God, Jesus, Buddha, or none of those but rather the experience in nature or the appreciation of music. Ishvara may have a personal meaning for you that does not resonate with anyone else.

Pranidhana is devotion or surrender. Put together ishvara pranidhana is more of an attitude of devotion you carry with you and live your life with. Can you see the divine in all and be open, humble, respectful, and peaceful? Can you incorporate a sense of spirituality into your life and work so it transcends the daily grind and elevates your contributions to become more meaningful and fulfilling? By practicing ishvara pranidhana we learn to shift our perspective from the obsession with "I" to a focus on the divine and others.

No matter what you may personally believe in or think of the Catholic Church, its current leader, Pope Francis, is enormously popular. His compassion, self-awareness, and accountability has shaped him into a standout leader who has become the "People's Pope." In just a few short years Pope Francis has chosen a transparent, non-pretentious approach to the papacy. He not only changed his own title from the "Supreme Pontiff" to the simpler "Bishop of Rome" but also reduced the hierarchy in his organization. Pope Francis models simplicity and humility from the inside out. He has a less opulent lifestyle than is customary and has notably informal interactions with people on the street or in a crowd. I was in New York City in September 2015, awaiting his arrival, when the pope first came to visit America. When he first arrived to the United States after landing in Washington, DC, he was escorted in a black Fiat 500 model. His official Popemobile (a word he does not like because it sets him too far apart from the people) for his US tour was a Jeep Wrangler. The Pope views his own behavior as essential to embodying the values he preaches. By modeling these values himself, he inspires his followers by showing them how they might embody the same values themselves.

You might think, *Hey, we're talking about the pope—shouldn't our expectations be very high for someone so elite?* Maybe, and certainly his decisions haven't pleased everyone. But we can all practice ishvara pranidhana to cultivate our ability and willingness to put aside our self-ish desires and let go of attachments, our need for control, and other self-imposed burdens.

Ben Chused of Sudbury, Massachusetts, is one of my favorite yoga instructors. Ben and I completed our three-hundred-hour teacher training together in 2015, and his calm, focus, discipline, and dedication to the practice inspired me. (And he had great tattoos and could do—and teach—all of the hard poses, like arm balances, which are my nemesis due to my tight hips!) By day Ben manages marketing campaigns at a major technology company, but he also teaches yoga on some evenings and weekends, primarily in the Boston area. And he is a husband and father of two kids. What's Ben's secret to juggling so many balls in the air? Ben tells me, "I remind myself every day that my true nature is to serve others. Whether it's my family, my coworkers, or my students, I believe I can improve their lives through service and devotion. If I surround myself with people who are content and can contribute to that contentment, it fulfills me." Through his teaching and his example Ben has helped me to find more peace, contentment, and joy in my own practice.

I spent Christmas of 2016 with my partner in London. During the day I enjoyed a brisk morning walk, soaked in the holiday atmosphere at Winter Wonderland in Hyde Park, and later we enjoyed a festive dinner at the iconic Soho restaurant Bob Bob Ricard. I awakened early the next morning to the sound of traffic outside the open window of my Portman Square hotel room. I could not get back to sleep and decided to hit the gym just before 6 a.m. I stepped onto the elliptical machine, turned the television to Bloomberg news, and quickly became engrossed in an interview with then eighty-three-year-old Supreme Court Justice Ruth Bader Ginsburg.

Ginsburg is known the world over as the Notorious RBG, a nickname that came from a Tumblr post in 2013 in tribute to her much-celebrated dissent to the court's attempt to strike down parts of the Voting Rights Act. Ginsberg, an aging icon of women's rights and equality, has become an even more popular cultural icon for the millennial generation. She is well known for her sharp and biting wit, her wisdom, and for being genuine.

In a 2016 *New York Times* piece Ginsburg relayed the guidance she received from her mother-in-law on her wedding day, which she now offers whenever asked for advice in public: "In every good marriage," she counseled, "it helps sometimes to be a little deaf." She continued, "I have followed that advice assiduously, and not only at home through 56 years of a marital partnership nonpareil. I have employed it as well in every workplace, including the Supreme Court. When a thoughtless or unkind word is spoken, best tune out. Reacting in anger or annoyance will not advance one's ability to persuade."

Having been in a relationship for over twenty-five years, I had to chuckle—but I realized how valuable her advice really was in any circumstance. Truly meaningful, successful leadership comes more from who you are on the inside rather than what you may do on the outside. By focusing on personal growth through a strong sense of self-discipline, you will lead by example, keep your team on track, and achieve your goals with the highest level of integrity, compassion, and the ability to adapt to any changing landscape. Even if your desk is a little messy.

Self-Reflection

1. Do you live with cleanliness of body, mind, and environment?

2. Are you satisfied with "what is," or are you always grasping for something more or different?

3. Why is self-discipline important in your life? What behaviors do you need to change to master self-discipline?

4. Are your thoughts, words, and behaviors aligned with your highest integrity?

5. Are you as you want to be?

6. How do you want others to see you?

7. Is your view of yourself congruent with others' views of you? Have you solicited feedback on how your are viewed by others?

8. Do you keep your efforts and rewards for yourself, or do you offer them up to others? To the divine?

3

Taking a Power Pose

"The study of asana is not about mastering posture.
It's about using posture to understand and
transform yourself."

—B. K. S. Iyengar

In ancient times yoga asanas were a means of enhancing the capacity of the body and mind to allow a person to sit in meditation for extended periods with as few distractions as possible. There is much more to yoga than the asanas, but there's no denying that the practice of these physical postures can offer profound mental and physical benefits, including steadiness, strength, flexibility, and lightness of limb. My yoga practice has helped me to manage stress while boosting my mental state in my work environment and beyond. The peace of mind I have found while actually performing the postures and deep stretches—yes, even at work!—has helped me to become a better leader by improving my mental clarity, building confidence, reducing stress, bolstering creativity, and supporting a stronger overall presence. And my practice has helped me to realize more joy—something I suspect we could all benefit from in any area of our lives.

We've all had days when we wake up on the wrong side of the bed, so to speak: our alarm fails to go off on time, our coffee is weak and seemingly without caffeine, our inbox is full of red-flag emails signaling urgent considerations that are often problems to address. Before we're even out the door we can hardly wait to crawl back into bed. (Last week I was in a rush and put both of my contact lenses in the same eye!) And I believe this is larger than just a personal hurdle. One of the many overarching challenges facing corporations today is that even the simplest decisions can require layer upon layer of discussion and approvals across the organization. How can we influence and contribute from within such a large bureaucratic structure? How can we stay grounded in the face of challenges and adversity that can often seem arbitrary, pointless, or self-inflicted? How can we cope with the stress of the continual uncertainty of organizational life? Bad days are inevitable, but it's how we address and manage what happens during those days that really matters.

The immediate goal of my personal practice is to quickly become centered through a short meditation and then to stay present during my asana practice. Whether I do one pose or twenty during each session, I:

1. maintain awareness of my breath,

2. maintain awareness of my base of support,

3. soften into the pose,

4. relax the parts of my body that are not engaged in the pose itself, and

5. observe without judgment.

All these skills support me as I transition into my day. Thus, I've become convinced that yoga is precisely what a very troubled corporate America needs today to face the challenges of tomorrow. When we have more space and stillness in our bodies, which will come from the practice of yoga and meditation, we experience more creativity, better focus, and new ideas that support our business success.

It may seem counterintuitive to *add* more activities to your to-do list, but the benefits of yoga and physical fitness are so profound that even a simple, five- or ten-minute practice can help you move through your days with greater energy and focus. If the words *Downward Facing Dog* or *Warrior 2* make you roll your eyes, this practice could be especially for you!

No, seriously. Eye rolling is actually one of several yoga poses to help relieve eyestrain. Most adult Americans spend more than ten hours per day staring at screens, including those on computer monitors, tablets, and smartphones. While many jobs require us to look at a computer screen most of the day, we then go home and relax by sitting at our computers and spending time on social media, reading news, watching sports, or playing games.

The overuse of computers has led to an increase in people who suffer from computer vision syndrome—a combination of eye and vision problems associated with the use of computers. Symptoms may include blurred vision, eyestrain, itchy and watery eyes, headaches, fatigue and other eye health issues. Simple exercises can help rejuvenate the eyes by resting overused muscles, reducing tension in the face and eyes, and helping to strengthen muscles that help the eyes focus.

Give Your Eyes a Break

The next time you realize you've been staring at a computer screen too long without stopping, take a break and try these simple exercises:

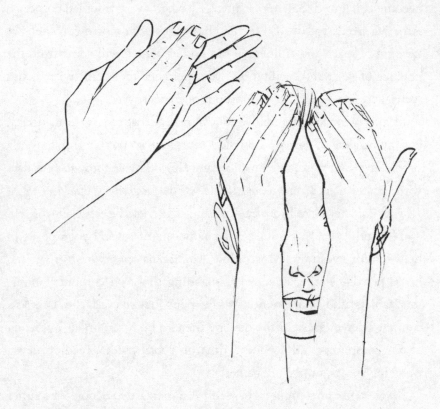

Palming

Rub your hands together for ten to twenty seconds until they feel warm and energized. Then gently place your hands over your closed eyes, with fingertips resting on the forehead, the palms over your eyes, and the heels of your hands resting on your cheeks. Don't touch your eyes directly but rather cup your hands around them. Feel and embrace the healing warmth and energy from your hands. Continue this palming action for as long as it feels soothing.

Eye Muscle Relaxation

Close your eyes as tightly as you possibly can. Really squeeze the eyes so the eye muscles contract. Hold this contraction for three seconds, and then let go quickly. This exercise causes a deep relaxation of the eye muscles.

Upward-Downward Gazing

Move your eyes upward as far as you can, and then downward as far as you can. Repeat four more times. Blink quickly a few times to relax your eye muscles.

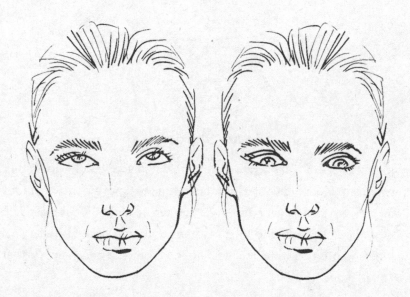

Focus Shifting

Sit upright or stand. Take a pencil, and hold it in your hand with an out-stretched arm. Keeping your eyes focused on the tip of a pencil (or index finger), move it toward your nose until you can no longer focus clearly on it. Pause for a moment, and then lengthen your arm back to its original outstretched position while maintaining focus on your pencil tip. Repeat five to ten times.

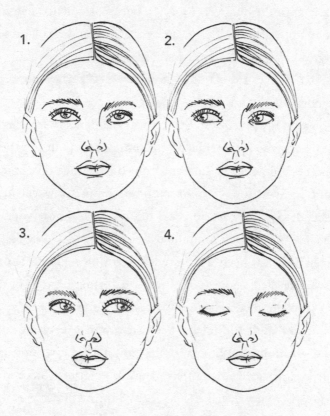

Eye Rolling

Sit upright. Soften your gaze by relaxing the muscles in your eyes and face. Without moving your head, direct your gaze up toward the ceiling. Slowly circle your eyes in a clockwise direction with a smooth and fluid movement, tracing as large a circle as possible. Repeat two to three times, then close your eyes and relax. Then perform the same eye-rolling movement two to three times in a counterclockwise direction.

Yoga is an individual practice. My personal practice has served to enhance my physical health and mental clarity and has led me to develop a greater spiritual connection. Despite my longstanding dedication to my practice, I don't strive to achieve a "perfect pose" (at least not anymore!), and you certainly don't have to either. I have learned not to compare my practice to that of other students in my classes or to fellow teachers who have achieved greater mastery than I in their asana practices. Yoga practice is different from other kinds of workouts. It's not about competition. It's not about opinions, physical fitness, or beauty standards. Yoga is a process of getting to know yourself, and each person's journey will be unique.

I haven't always been a devoted practitioner—in fact, for many years I was skeptical about yoga. I met my former partner in the mid-1980s. We were and continue to be very different people. For the entirety of my adult life I have been involved in a variety of fitness endeavors—running, hiking, weight training, cycling, and triathlon training. He, however, has intermittently practiced meditation and yoga for over twenty years. When I saw him meditating early in our relationship I couldn't understand how anyone would want to sit on a floor with his eyes closed and breathe—at the time I thought this looked rather silly, and there were so many better and more fun things to do! Furthermore, I didn't appreciate why anyone would want to do an asana practice, as there seemed to be so many more effective ways to achieve your fitness goals. He told me that these practices were very helpful for focus and reducing stress; I remained a nonbeliever.

Then, starting around fifteen years ago, my life circumstances changed and became very difficult for me to manage. I was faced with serious issues at home. I then navigated a shift in my career from a focus in academic medicine to my first job in the pharmaceutical industry in 2006. This transition meant relocating from Texas to Connecticut. Shortly after moving, my father, a trusted source of love, support, and guidance, was diagnosed with advanced kidney cancer and died six months later. I felt helpless and, at times, hopeless. I tried to take care of myself through all of this, but I seemed to be falling short with my focus on exercise, nutrition, family, and work. I felt unstable through all these changes and sought the advice of a therapist, which failed to improve the situation. (I am a believer in the benefits of psychotherapy, but in this case it was not effective.) It became clear that I needed something else.

I am a survivor. Every October since my diagnosis in 1993 I mark the anniversary of another year free of thyroid cancer! Wow—it's been over twenty-four years! I have also worked with cancer patients and survivors throughout my career and recognize that curing disease is not enough—the goal is not only to cure disease but also to ensure quality of survival. This very quality hinges on attitude, courage, and strength. I had read that yoga could help foster these attributes in cancer patients, so what did I have to lose?

I began the practice of yoga on a whim. Being a book geek and a bookstore junkie, I searched and read all I could find about the philosophy of yoga in addition to taking a variety of public classes mostly focused on asana. I slowly began to feel more grounded as a person and in my work, no longer so easily riled or reactive. The operative word here is *slowly*. Over several years I developed a sense of inner calm and outer stability. I enjoyed the yoga community, which was more cosmopolitan than my professional community, and I learned to better internalize our oneness as a society.

After more than a decade of practice I have greater insight, clarity, and acuity, all of which inform my leadership style. In earlier years I was fiercely independent and had a view that I could do everything myself. I knew I was smart, motivated, and driven, and I felt that I did not really need other people. Now I strive to lead through my passion, energy, and with a positive attitude. I desire to encourage creativity, listen, reflect, and communicate well. I am no longer personally challenged by the power of my superiors. And I recognize the value of a team approach and the unique and vital contributions of each member of the team. I encourage and support my team members to excel in their work and then recognize them for their efforts. People matter—they are *the key* to organizational success.

I generally start my day with both a fitness workout and a short asana practice. Every day, when I first get out of bed, I do a three- to five-minute seated meditation to center myself and prepare mindfully for the day. Five or six days a week I head to my local gym, where I usually spend about an hour doing a combination of cardio exercises, strength training, yoga postures, and stretches. My routine may sound like a lot of work, but in truth it's become as natural as brushing my teeth—it's how I start my day. (Most days, anyway. There are a few days when I decide to stay in bed and sleep an hour longer. Sleep is important too!)

Because this routine is so important to me, I always pack my yoga/fitness clothing whenever I travel. My motto? If I don't have it, I can't use it. Keeping scheduled appointments and dressing the part—my "suit" for working out, so to speak—motivates me to take my physical practice seriously. I also like to reward myself after a good workout with a strong coffee (I like a café Americano with three shots of expresso!), a healthy breakfast, and a hot shower. Then I feel ready to take on most anything that day.

My early-morning routine may not be for everyone, but I've found that making it a habit to begin my day with a sweat-inducing workout and short yoga practice almost always leads to a productive, effective day—I am more relaxed, adaptable, and resilient to whatever the day throws at me. If you're not a morning person, you can still reap the benefits of a yoga practice anytime it's most convenient—in your office (see pages 82–86 for some starter routines) after morning meetings, at lunchtime, during an afternoon lull, or perhaps even before bed if you have time to yourself in the evenings. Depending on the time of day, you may want to focus on different postures to create a specific mood; for example, in the evenings perhaps you choose more relaxing, restorative poses. When you have the time and if you have the interest, I recommend you seek out a yoga studio near you. Practicing initially with the guidance of a certified yoga instructor is a good way to make sure you are doing each pose with good alignment to avoid injury. If being a beginner makes you hesitate, don't feel intimidated! Both yoga students and yoga teachers are generally nonjudgmental and welcoming. I love the sense of community that I find at almost all the yoga studios throughout the country.

No matter when you practice, you can be sure the physical practice and breathing exercises will help you let go of daily distractions, center your mind, and feel stronger, taller, and more confident.

Among leaders poise, charisma, passion, and an unfailingly genuine personality often take precedence over skill or originality—you could call all these things *presence*. In her book *Presence: Bringing Your Boldest Self to Your Biggest Challenges*, social psychologist Amy Cuddy writes that "presence manifests as confidence without arrogance," and she suggests an adaptation of the old adage, "fake it 'til you make it": fake it 'til you become it. Her idea is simple: by assuming a physical pose associated with power, you can actually make yourself *feel* more powerful and confident before an important event, such as a business meeting or a presentation. Cuddy asserts that power posing inspires you to be more authentic, more passionate, and more present, thereby enabling you to show your worth with greater ease and conviction.

When I first started yoga I didn't feel all that powerful while practicing my poses. I never felt I had enough time. I would be in the middle of a class holding a pose, with my mind racing through my to-do list: *After class I need to go to the grocery store, fill up my gas tank, and then go home to return phone calls, check email, and pay some bills. Maybe I can save time by returning one or two of the calls while I fill up my gas tank. I'll just hit the mute button if there is any background noise.* Sound familiar? I would move from pose to pose, struggling to keep focused, often feeling heavy, tight, and anxious.

Finally I decided to try something different. Yoga teachers often suggest that students "surrender." It was initially difficult for me to understand this yoga-speak. I don't easily give up or, worse, settle for anything. But the word *surrender* in yoga means none of those things. It is a letting go—a releasing of the thoughts, worries, and fears that keep us from receiving the gifts of relaxation and rejuvenation. So I let go of my struggle and surrendered, and I began to transition from pose to pose, focusing only on my breathing and my movements. Soon thereafter my yoga practice opened a new way of being in time.

By changing my intentions, my to-do list floated away, and I developed the ability to stay in the current moment of body, breath, movement, sweat, and gaze. From this place I have enhanced my presence in a way that has transcended my yoga class. I've adopted a stronger stance as I go about my daily routine, as well as a greater openness in both my personal and professional life.

As she reflected on teaching at Harvard Business School, Cuddy acknowledged that she'd been pretending to be confident until she actually felt confident. Do most people doubt themselves and feel like imposters? I've certainly had such doubts myself. My solution has been to practice yoga, which helps me live more authentically, powerfully, and with genuine presence.

Mighty Movements

After sitting eight hours a day in an office and then walking a short distance to a train or your car, all while staring at your smartphone, you're totally misaligning your spine. Did you know that yoga postures that target areas of tension can be an effective antidote to many desk-job ailments? Simple yoga-inspired movements are the best remedy for a stiff, sore neck and shoulders if you've been in the same position for a while—whether at your desk, in front of a screen, in your car, or while traveling.

Here's a short sequence you can do in a few minutes at the office to release tension in your neck and shoulders. Practicing a few poses and short sequences throughout the day can make a big difference in how you feel at work, which may translate into greater contentment and productivity.

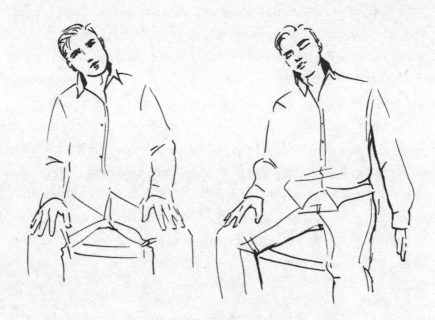

Lateral Neck Stretches

Start by warming up with a few breaths, feeling the movement of inhalation and exhalation.

Sitting upright on the edge of a chair or standing, tilt your head to the right as if your right ear might touch your right shoulder (but keep your shoulders down). Extend your left arm and hand down, with your fingers pointing toward the ground, until you feel a deep stretch on the left side of your neck. Breathe deeply, holding the stretch for a few breath cycles, then repeat on the other side.

Seated Clasping Neck and
Between-the-Shoulders Stretch

Sitting straight in a chair with a long spine, ground your hips firmly onto your seat. Clasp your hands, and bring both palms to the back of your head. Gently press your elbows down, tucking your chin toward your chest and using your hands to gently pull your head away from your shoulders. Hold for at least thirty seconds, and then slowly lift your head up and release your hands. Repeat three to five times.

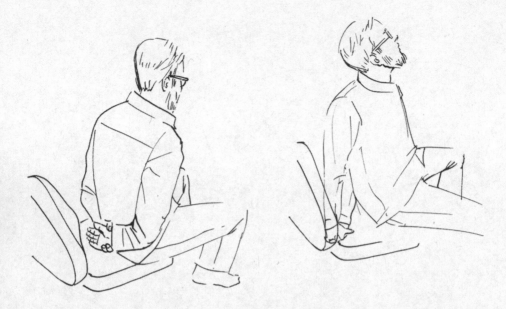

Reverse Arch Stretch

This stretch opens the chest, shoulders, and front of your neck. Sit on the edge of your chair. Reach your hands behind you, and clasp them together, or hold on to the back of the chair, with your fingers pointing down toward the floor. Press your chest forward, arching your spine. If it feels comfortable, let your head fall back slightly to open through the front of the neck. Feel the front of your body open as you extend backward. Hold this position for twenty to thirty seconds, and don't forget to breathe. Then slowly lift your head up, straighten your spine, and release your hold of the chair.

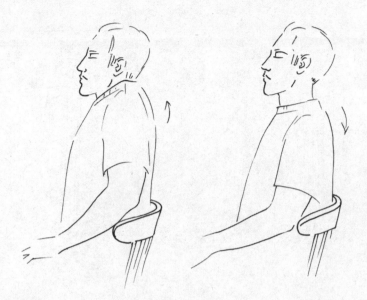

Shoulder Rolls

Sit on the edge of a chair. Bend your knees and place your feet hip-width apart on the floor. Shift your hips until you feel both sitz bones (sitting bones, or the base of your pelvis) press equally into the seat. Sit up straight with a long spine. Your neck should align with your spine so your head is over the center of your shoulders and your chin is level to the floor and not jutting forward. Lift your right shoulder up toward your ear, and then roll it forward and down. Next, lift your left shoulder roll up toward your ear, then forward and down. Alternate rolls in this direction until each shoulder has rolled three times. Next, roll your shoulders in the opposite direction (up, backward, and down) three times each. Finish by inhaling as you lift both shoulders together up to the ears. Exhale as you quickly release them. Repeat five times to relax your shoulders.

Doorway Stretch
(Underarms and Anterior Shoulders)

Stand upright in a doorway, feet shoulder-width apart. Slowly lift your arms, and place your palms on the door frame so your arms resemble the letter "U." Take a step forward. Then slowly and gently lean your upper body forward. When you feel a stretch in your underarm and chest area, hold that stretch for twenty seconds while breathing comfortably. Slowly return your body to the original position. Relax ten seconds.

   Note: If a doorway is not available, you also can do this exercise while facing the corner of two adjacent walls.

Job stress creates up to 60 percent of employee absenteeism and costs employers more than $200 billion each year in absenteeism, tardiness, burnout, lower productivity, high turnover, worker's compensation, and medical insurance costs, according to the National Safety Council. Stress shuts down the sort of creative thinking that can generate profitable ideas. According to a 2014 Monster.com survey, 42 percent of workers have left a job due to a stressful environment, and another 35 percent have considered changing jobs due to stress.

But some of America's healthiest companies are now creating a culture of wellness, proving that employees' health, happiness, and work-life balance are vital to their own success—fewer employee absences, lower healthcare costs, and higher overall morale encourages employees to stick around for the long haul. Innovative employers generally agree that if you invest in employees' growth and development, they will do a better job for the company.

At Green Mountain Coffee Roasters in Waterbury, Vermont, workers begin shifts with "mindful movement" sessions designed to help them clear their minds of distractions so they can focus on the task at hand. Even the factories where the coffee is packaged have meditation rooms. Linda Marshall, president of the WebLyn Group, an independent consultancy that provides strategic direction to companies in the telecommunications, wireless, and healthcare industries, built yoga centers while working at both Nextel Communications and OnStar, a subsidiary of General Motors. In a *New York Times* article in 2011, during her tenure as president of OnStar, Marshall said, "I work hard, but I believe in balance. I've been practicing yoga for thirteen years, and I teach it. Yoga is about simplicity and focus, and it contributes to wellness." Google has been a leader in encouraging yoga and meditation in the workplace. These practices go hand in hand. "Meditation skills can help staffers be happier and become better leaders," says mindfulness meditation teacher Marc Lesser, co-founder and former CEO of the Search Inside Yourself Leadership Institute, which offers a two-day course in which participants develop the knowledge and learn skills to embrace the benefits of mindfulness, emotional intelligence, and compassionate leadership and subsequently are poised to bring these benefits into the workplace. Lesser states, "We work hard to have meaningful work and a meaningful life. The underlying question is, What really matters? And, How can I live in a way that helps others, and how can I be part of creating social change?"

Several times a year, I participate in national and international scientific meetings as a speaker or facilitator, and it is imperative that I am attuned to the needs of the audience. It's not something they teach in medical school but certainly something I have learned through my practice of yoga. I admit that some of the material presented at these meetings is dry. I need to be especially creative when my session is after lunch, which is the most dreaded time to speak—stomachs are full, blood flow is diverted to digestion, and minds are drifting. How do I help the audience to regain focus and make sure their comprehension is maximized when all they want to do is close their eyes and snooze?

If you guessed yoga, well, it wasn't much of a trick question! I typically take two to three minutes before the start of a session to ask the audience to join me in a few cycles of slow, conscious breathing while seated (see Chapter 4). Next I might have everyone stand up with their feet hip-width apart, shoulders drawn back, chests lifted, chins up, abdomens pulled in, while we practice some gentle neck stretches and arm movements. This helps participants feel grounded and release tension in their necks, arms, and upper backs. Short, sweet, effective. And then we begin. Please feel free to copy this approach whenever you have a captive audience who seems a little less than enthusiastic—I promise in no time you'll feel more connected, empowered, and effective in delivering your message as a true leader.

Mark Bertolini, CEO of Aetna, suffered a broken neck in a skiing accident over a decade ago. He broke his neck in five places and lost the use of one arm. His pain was so severe that it led him to search for any therapy that might provide relief. Bertolini chose to manage his pain without narcotics; this is how he stumbled into yoga and meditation. He found it so helpful that he eventually made meditation and yoga classes available to all employees at Aetna. In 2010 the medical insurance company determined that workers in its most stress-prone positions were racking up medical bills that exceeded those of other employees by an average of $2,000 per year. In 2012 Aetna reduced its healthcare costs by 7 percent—a savings Bertolini pegs in part to limiting stress through meditation and yoga.

Richard Davidson, a neuroscientist at the University of Wisconsin-Madison, is the founder of the Center for Healthy Minds. Davidson has emerged as an authority in studying the effects of well-being practices, such as breathing and practicing compassion, in schools and in the business world. Davidson says, "In the workplace, we think these kinds of strategies improve efficiency, improve attention, fostering emotional balance, facilitating interpersonal interest and teamwork and cooperative activities more generally."

In yoga, movement, breath, and body are synchronized. Yoga teaches you to channel your breath and focus your mind clearly on the present, prioritizing what is most important at that moment. The ability to slow down the mind leads to a more rational thinking and expansive awareness; you will enhance your problem-solving abilities and begin to envision a variety of new ideas and solutions to everyday problems. Yoga enhances creativity, teaches us balance, and helps us more effectively recognize and explore options with greater openness and

Yoga Can Make
Your Workplace Better

Maybe the word *yoga* still sounds a little too hippy-dippy for your corporate headquarters. But what if your company was offered the opportunity to teach its employees an essential skill that anyone, no matter what level, could be proficient in to be more productive? Let's look at it from a business perspective.

1. Reduces absenteeism and illness

    - Supports employees in managing stress and/or depression/anxiety

    - Helps moderate reactions to and perceptions of stress

    - Decreases the need for time off due to illness

    - Reduces the risk of acute and chronic medical conditions

    - Increases physical energy and vitality

    - Reduces pain from repetitive injuries and chronic conditions

2. Increases productivity and morale

    - Improves concentration

    - Enhances focus and creative thinking

    - Increases energy and reduces fatigue

    - Improves alertness and the ability to react more calmly in demanding situations

    - Improves employee attitude and outlook

3. Decreases workplace injuries

  ≥ Improves posture and flexibility

  ≥ Improves balance, concentration, and strength

If someone handed you this list and said your employees or co-workers could achieve these benefits simply from doing thirty minutes of daily exercises right in their workplace, wouldn't you want to implement this program immediately? You can—and it's called yoga.

flexibility while also balancing multiple responsibilities. Whether you're leading a team of employees or learning to prioritize your own workload, yoga supports stronger leadership and effectiveness.

Bringing yoga to your own workplace uniquely positions companies to support both your employees' well-being and the corporate bottom line. Happy and healthy people are more productive, creative and innovative employees who exude positivity and self-confidence. The bottom line: practicing yoga is a proactive strategy to live well, be well, and stay well.

How many hours do you sit—or, rather, slouch—in meetings or at your desk? Most of us tend to sit forward with slumped shoulders, our heads dropped. Smartphones, laptops, desk jobs, and long commutes all contribute to making us look like we are chronically hunched over. What about lunch time? Do you find yourself slouching at your desk while shoveling your salad or chomping your sandwich in the five minutes (or less) available prior to your next meeting? We've become so accustomed to this posture that, chances are, we don't even notice it. Perhaps you've been shocked by a photo of yourself looking hunched or slumped—and not particularly happy or confident. Poor posture isn't just unattractive; it can also be extremely painful, causing tightness, aches, and soreness around the neck, shoulders, and upper and lower back. (By the way, back pain is the top reason for physician visits in the United States.)

Improving your posture with yoga requires you to breathe while doing poses that open your chest and shoulders, allow you to gently bend your back, and lengthen your spine. A regular yoga practice will help you experience what a steady, balanced posture feels like.

Try these six relatively simple yet challenging poses that you can do anytime during the day to improve your posture. You can pick and choose whichever appeals to you at that moment and don't need to do them in any particular order. Mountain pose and the standing forward bend don't even require a change of clothes (except perhaps removing your shoes).

The illustrations that accompany these images are intended to help you get a general feel for each pose; read the instructions well. However, there are variations of these poses and different ways to flow between the movements. If you are interested in deepening your asana practice and learning more about these and many other movements available to you, I recommend you seek out *Ashtanga Yoga: The Practice Manual* by David Swenson—one of my favorite manuals—or another guide that speaks to you.

Remember that poor posture develops over time, so good posture takes time to build back up as well. Determine which of these poses resonates with you, and try practicing them daily, gradually increasing the time in each pose. You should find improvement in your posture.

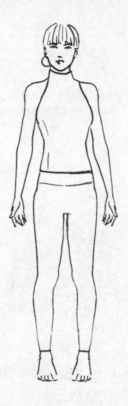

Mountain Pose
(Tadasana)

Tadasana is really how we should be standing all the time. Stand tall, with your feet about hip-distance apart and parallel to each other. Open your chest by rolling your shoulders back and down to lower your shoulder blades. Have your arms at your sides, palms facing forward. Align your head so your chin is parallel to the floor and the crown of your head is directly over the center of your pelvis. Engage your core and thighs, and slightly tuck your tailbone. Breathe. Stay in the pose for at least thirty seconds. This pose may not feel like much, but it is a very active pose, as it requires your whole body to be engaged. Once you've got it, develop an awareness of your body habitus in this pose. Start walking naturally, but keep your shoulders back and down and your chin neutral, level to the ground.

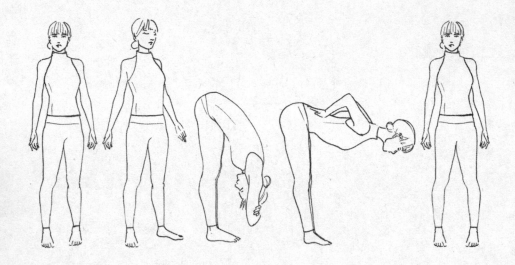

Standing Forward Bend
(Uttanasana)

Stand in Mountain Pose, exhale, and bend forward from the hip joints, not the waist. Cross your forearms, and hold your elbows with opposite hands. Press your heels into the ground, your knees straight (be careful not to lock them back), and lift your sitz bones toward the ceiling. The emphasis is on lengthening the front torso while relaxing the neck and head as you move more fully into the position. With each inhalation in the pose, lift and lengthen the front torso slightly, with each exhalation release more fully into the forward bend. Stay in the pose for at least thirty seconds. To release the pose, place your hands on your hips, and reaffirm the length of the front torso. Rise on an inhalation with the long front torso. This pose calms the mind and helps relieve stress, anxiety, fatigue, and tension in the spine, neck, and back.

Can you feel your spine lengthen as you fold over toward your feet? (This pose may save visits to a chiropractor!)

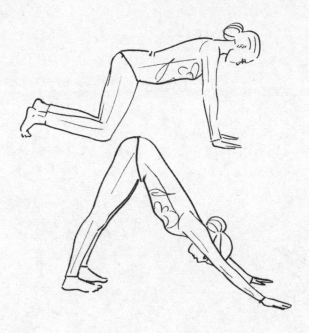

Downward Facing Dog
(Adho Muka Svanasana)

Come onto the floor on your hands and knees. Place your knees directly below your hips and your hands slightly forward of your shoulders. Spread your fingers wide, and press firmly through your palms and knuckles. Exhale as you tuck your toes, lift your knees off the floor, and slowly work to straighten your legs (they may not fully straighten). Press the floor away from you as you lift through your pelvis, hips toward the ceiling. Adjust your hands forward a bit if necessary while keeping your spine long and your head and neck loose, in line with your spine. Hold for at least thirty seconds. This is a great pose for improving your posture, as it stretches and lengthens the spine and opens your shoulders. Downward Facing Dog is an inversion, so it increases the flow of blood to the brain while calming the nervous system, thus helping you relax and clear your head.

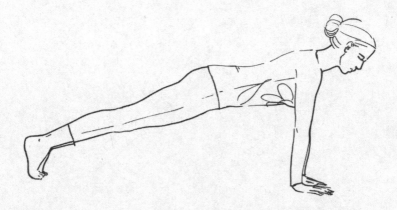

Plank Pose

Start in Downward Facing Dog. Inhale and draw your torso forward until your arms are perpendicular to the floor and your shoulders are directly over your wrists. Adjust your feet as needed to make sure your wrists are underneath your shoulders. Your hands should be open and parallel. Press the base of your index fingers and thumbs into the floor. Press your shoulder blades together. Keep your head, neck, and torso parallel to the floor. Hold for up to one minute. Don't forget to breathe.

Sometimes slouching stems from having a weak core that lacks the strength to hold us upright. Plank Pose will strengthen your core, which will take some of the stress off your spine, allowing you to hold yourself up straight with greater ease.

Cobra Pose (Bhujangasana)

Lie prone on the floor, stretch your legs back, keep them together, and place your hands with palms down and under your shoulders, fingertips facing forward. Hug your elbows back into your body. Press the tops of your feet, thighs, and pubis firmly into the floor. On an inhalation, slowly straighten your arms to lift your chest off the floor, going only to a height at which you can maintain a connection to the floor from your pubis to your legs. Traction your hands on the mat, pulling back, while pulling forward with your chest and lifting your gaze. Bring your shoulders away from your ears while keeping your pelvis and toes on the mat. Hold for a few breaths (ten to twenty seconds). Release back to the floor with an exhalation. Repeat three times. This pose is a backbend and is an ideal pose for strengthening your back and opening your chest.

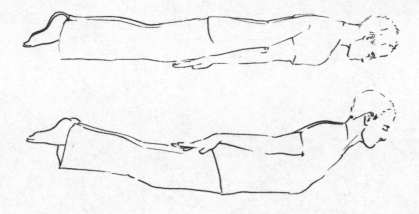

Locust Pose (Salabhasana)

Lie on your belly, with your legs long and arms extended along the sides of your torso, palms facing down and forehead resting on the floor. On an exhale, lift your head, upper torso, arms, and legs away from the floor. You will be resting on your lower ribs, belly, and front pelvis. Gently firm (don't squeeze) your buttocks, and reach strongly through your legs. Internally rotate your thighs, keeping the big toes turned toward each other. Roll your shoulder blades back to open your chest. Gaze slightly forward, careful not to jut your chin forward. Keep the base of your skull lifted and the back of your neck long. Remember to breathe. Hold for ten to twenty seconds, and then release with an exhalation. Repeat two times. (There are several variations of this pose; I have described the one that I find most effective.) This pose is a backbend, which serves to open the chest and strengthen the back.

So many of us dread the thought of speaking in front of others, whether it's a weekly staff meeting or a large-scale presentation. Of course, I am not suggesting you move into Downward Facing Dog during a business meeting—although many companies have now adopted "walking meetings" intended to promote active conversation! But when faced with the need to speak in public, our anxiety and fears can often overtake us and prevent us from connecting with our audience and communicating effectively. Think of the last great speech you attended—what was the speaker doing that made him seem so engaging and interesting? Chances are he spoke with a strong, confident presence, delivering his message with purpose and clarity. You can do this too with a few simple exercises.

When speaking in front of others it's critical to maintain a strong presence. You are—or you should be—the center of everyone's attention. By staying focused, alert, and engaged, you will encourage your audience to do the same, ensuring they hear you loud and clear and, more importantly, remember what you've said.

Here are a few ways you can use yogic elements to help improve your ability to speak in front of others, project confidence, and capture their attention.

1. Your balance in some yoga poses is enhanced by use of a *drishti*, or focal point. By focusing on a drishti during a pose, your mind is better able to balance in concert with your body. Consider your presentation topic as a drishti— something easy to focus on and smooth to deliver. If you have anxiety before or during a presentation, you may want to focus on one object or a friendly face in the room, which will help you feel calmer and speak more slowly and with a greater connection to your audience.

2. Stand with your feet hip width apart. Keep your spine lengthened and straight, and engage your core muscles. Good speakers are stable and grounded with a strong connection to their core. Yoga will help you gain body awareness and lead to improved posture. It will also help you speak from a self-assured place so your audience will perceive you as confident and knowledgeable.

3. Periodically pause and take a breath. Breathe in through the nose and out through the nose. This will help to keep you calm, focused, and well paced so you don't rush through the presentation. It will also keep your audience interested in the next thing you have to say.

4. Recall how you felt after listening to a presenter drone on and on while flipping through endless PowerPoint slides— exhausted. Yoga empowers communication. Diversify your tone and delivery style during a presentation. No death by slide shows, please.

Recognizing the value of being in the moment is especially useful during meetings, when others are depending on you to be an attentive listener and observer as well as an active participant.

We are all affected by stress and anxiety on a daily basis. I know I've had some difficult days I'd rather forget! Now, using the yoga postures and techniques I have shared in this chapter, I react to even the greatest stressors differently, with greater calm and ease. I am able to leave the emotion around work-related issues behind when I walk out the door and show up for the rest of my life with a more positive outlook. Before practicing yoga my glass was often half empty—and it is now usually half full. That's quite a powerful shift from a deceptively simple philosophy.

Yoga has also taught me to laugh at myself. When I first started my yoga practice I tried to do every posture perfectly and got upset when I could not. The difference between then and now is that when everything goes completely wrong and I fall out the postures or fail entirely, I don't get upset (well, not for more than a few seconds)—I find ways to laugh. After all, it's only yoga.

Self-Reflection

During your yoga practice ask yourself:

1. How am I feeling today?

2. Is my attention focused on my body and breath, or is it elsewhere?

3. Am I experiencing any physical pain?

4. When I have a thought, can I let it go?

5. What is the quality of my breath?

6. What is my state of mind?

7. At the conclusion of practice: Has anything shifted for me?

4

Breathing
through Life's Challenges

*"When the breath wanders the mind also is
unsteady. But when the breath is calmed the mind
too will be still, and the yogi achieves long life.
Therefore, one should learn to control the breath."*

—Svatmarama, Hatha Yoga Pradipika

I arrived in Boston on the eve of St. Patrick's Day 2016 to deliver an important lecture at our manufacturing facility in northern Massachusetts. My colleague Michael and I had been given an opportunity by the head of the site to showcase our entire program and the depth of our collaborative efforts; the entire staff was invited. We had prepared for months, and I was excited to share the work of our team so broadly.

I had a little trouble sleeping that night, as loud celebrations leading up to the city's famous Irish heritage parades and festivities continued into the wee hours of the morning. Nevertheless, after a morning workout and short meditation I felt refreshed and ready to go. I did my typical routine (see Chapter 3), starting with seated breathing, followed by gentle yoga poses to help limber up my body, and then a thirty-minute run on the treadmill. This may sound a bit daunting, but I've done this type of morning ritual for over twenty-five years, and it has actually become a pleasurable habit. I generally feel great at the end of my workout, and I usually meet the challenges of the rest of my day with greater focus and ease.

About five minutes before I was due on stage I felt my briefcase that was next to me vibrating—my personal phone was buzzing with calls and text messages. This was highly unusual, especially during daytime hours, as my friends and family respect my working hours and typically try to reach me only in the evenings. I felt both anxiety and curiosity welling up inside of me as I pulled my phone out of my briefcase—I had two missed calls and five text messages from my son.

"Call me urgently. I need to talk to you," they read. Now I felt a wave of panic overcome me. *What was wrong?* I quickly sent him a text: "Are you okay? Can I call you in an hour?" He responded yes and that he would be waiting for my call. I knew my son would be honest if he needed my attention immediately, so I tried to suspend my anxiety, worry, and fear—my head and heart were both pounding, and I felt panicky and short of breath.

I had to get calm and focused—*fast*—as I was about to step on stage. I had done so much preparation for this lecture and wanted to make a great impression in support of my team's efforts, not betray my inner alarm bells!

Instead of losing control and letting my inner thoughts overtake me, I focused on my breathing, calmed my mind, and shifted my focus back to the present situation. In just a few short minutes I gathered my composure, quickly got in sync with Michael, and we delivered a flawless—well, in my opinion!—lecture and discussion session. I called my son immediately thereafter, and he had handled a difficult situation at home very well—things were generally okay.

And the feedback we received after our presentation was great! I was relieved on all accounts.

If you've ever missed a critical deadline or found out your company was planning a merger or unexpectedly going out of business, you've likely experienced the way your thoughts and fears (mind) can affect your breathing (body). When life's unexpected surprises come our way our lungs often seem to seize up, just as mine did before my presentation.

In Sanskrit *prana* means breath. More fundamentally it means energy, strength, vitality—the life force that holds all things together. *Pranayama* connotes the expansion of breath and its control and fosters the development of breath as a tool for vital living. Prana is a powerful force. It is considered the integrating principle of all life. A smooth, free, and undisturbed flow of prana supports good health and ease of body and mind. When we can center our awareness and flow of prana in a single direction, we can achieve the kind of concentration, focus, and clarity necessary to function optimally in our work.

In the yoga sutras Patañjali described our ability to control prana as a matter of regulating our inhalation and exhalation as well as the pause between breaths. This method of focused breathing is the practice of pranayama, a specific, intentional way of inhaling and exhaling over a period of time to produce a desired effect on your body and mind. In Sanskrit the suffix *-ayama* means to lengthen, stretch, or extend. Thus, pranayama can be considered the conscious expansion of our natural capacity for breath. The aim of pranayama is to foster a free and undisturbed flow of prana so we can quiet and calm our minds and focus successfully on the task at hand.

How often do you think about breathing? On average a person at rest takes about 16 breaths per minute. This means we breathe about 960 breaths an hour, 23,040 breaths a day, and 8,409,600 breaths a year. Unfortunately, in the modern world most of us have lost touch with our breath. We operate under constant stress, spend hours hunched over a computer keyboard, and wear tight clothing that restricts our ability to relax, open up, and breathe optimally. Optimal breathing is a full, free, and uninhibited breath from the diaphragm, one that fills our lungs, oxygenates our blood, and energizes us. Think of the last time you took a full, conscious breath from deep in your belly—or maybe you just did! You'll learn a few simple breathing techniques in this chapter that will help you better connect with your prana and reap the benefits in just minutes.

When we are stressed, fearful, or hear bad news we often gasp—inhaling sharply and then holding our breath. These breathing patterns can activate the sympathetic nervous system, often referred to as the "fight or flight response." Pranayama is meant to expand, intensify, and consolidate the energies of the breath by directing, regulating, and balancing their flow. This process helps us break our unconscious breathing patterns and make the breath long, easeful, and smooth. Our unconscious breathing patterns are generally not easeful and smooth; like a gasp, they tend to be tense, shallow, and erratic.

Have you ever heard the advice to "just breathe" when you're stressed? Although a well-known cliché, it's true. Pranayama techniques can support the parasympathetic nervous system and activate what is commonly known as the "relaxation response," which reduces stress and its negative effects on the mind and body. As a result, we gain greater resilience in the face of adversity, and our minds become less cluttered and frantic.

In the yoga sutras, Patañjali writes, "As a result [of pranayama], the covering that blocks our own inner light is reduced." In other words, through the practice of pranayama you can reduce mental noise—the agitation, distractions, and self-doubt—that prevents you from connecting with your true self and reaching your full potential.

As a leader I rely on breath control throughout my day, especially in challenging situations. It's an essential survival tool. If I feel overwhelmed or am coming out of a tense meeting and need to clear my head, a few minutes of deep breathing helps me achieve balance. In my experience there are two basic types of stressful situations: (1) ongoing, predictable job stressors like meeting deadlines or juggling multiple projects at once and (2) sudden crises that happen unexpectedly, like hearing your company is downsizing or your boss is changing (of course, this can be good or bad, depending upon how you feel about your boss!). And stress is not just a workplace phenomenon; we experience stressful situations throughout our lives—the kids won't stop screaming, your partner has unrealistic demands, or your bills are mounting up and you don't have the money to pay them. Sound familiar?

The contemporary business world has often been described as a combative, competitive war, one in which leaders are quite literally fighting for their very survival, let alone the possibility of growth. The business war is complex and uncertain at best and, at worst, turbulent and volatile. It likely comes as no surprise that leaders are under significantly more pressure than the average employee and, at times, may feel unable to stop the pressure from overtaking them. Stress and corporate life go hand in hand. The cost to American industry for stress-induced loss of effectiveness and efficiency is over US$300 billion per year. (Did you read that figure twice?) Most leaders have reported at some point feeling any combination of sleeplessness, depression, anxiety, tension, fear, and somatic illness. Perhaps you have too.

Even a leader who, under optimal circumstances, is seen as effective, dedicated, thoughtful, and at ease may be perceived as tense, disengaged, erratic, and angry under pressure. This shifting perception can quickly lead to a lack of support and engagement, and it could sabotage his success.

Medical studies have demonstrated that there is a powerful connection between your breath and your ability to handle stress. Slow, deep breaths that engage the abdominal muscles and diaphragm, instead of the muscles in your upper chest and neck, can bring you back from the emotional brink in even the worst situations. Military officers implement tactical breathing techniques (see page 111) to help regain control of their bodies and minds during critical situations. Rhythmic patterns of breath also strengthen the respiratory system and soothe the nervous system. Deep breathing triggers the parasympathetic nervous system linked to stimulation of the vagus nerve, which runs from the base of the brain to the abdomen and is responsible for mediating nervous system responses and lowering your heart rate, among other things. Thus, deep breathing is one of the most efficient ways to focus on the present, center yourself, and feel relaxed, thereby reducing stress and anxiety, even in the most challenging moments. When you breathe deeply, it sends a message to your brain to calm down and relax. The brain then sends this message to your body. Those things that happen when you are stressed, such as increased heart rate, fast breathing, elevated blood sugar, and high blood pressure, all decrease as you breathe deeply to relax.

It takes a little practice to integrate proper breathing into your daily life, but the effort is worth it: by training your body with a regular practice of deep breathing you will begin to breathe more effectively automatically. Regular practitioners of yoga can exert a strong influence over their thoughts and emotions through proper breath control.

Grow Your Brain

One of the more intriguing research developments involving diaphragmatic breathing is that when it's used to facilitate meditation, the result can be an actual increase in brain size. As evaluated by magnetic resonance imaging, the brain experiences growth in areas associated with attention and processing of sensory input. The effect seems to be more noticeable in older people, which is especially good news because it's the reverse of what typically happens as we age—gray matter usually becomes thinner. (We'll return to meditation in Chapter 8.)

These simple, easy-to-follow breathing exercises take just a few minutes, and they will help reduce stress and anxiety, promote restful sleep, increase attention and focus, and, on a subtle level, help you connect to a calm, quiet place within. Try to practice breath control on a daily basis, and you'll quickly start to notice a greater clarity and sense of well-being.

Observing Your Breath

Prior to beginning these breathing techniques observe your breath as it is.

≥ Sit on a chair in a comfortable position with your spine erect and your feet flat on the floor, about hip-distance apart. Close your eyes. Breathe naturally and comfortably for a few moments, through your nose only, noticing the quality of your breath. Does it feel strained? Tense? Irregular? Shallow? What sensations accompany your breathing? Do you know when your breath is shallow or what makes it speed up? Simply becoming aware of your breath tends to slow your breathing rate down.

> Observe your breath without any judgment. Awareness is the key to transformation. Attempting to "correct" your breath simply imposes another pattern. Instead, witness your breath as it is.

Diaphragmatic Breathing

Diaphragmatic breathing has long been a feature of Eastern health practices, as it helps you breathe more fully and consciously. By focusing on your breath you will quiet and calm your nervous system, thus reducing stress and anxiety and improving self-awareness. It's such a simple exercise that you can try it at least once a day, at any time of day or evening (see page 113).

How to do it:

> Sit on a chair in a comfortable position with your spine erect and your feet flat on the floor, about hip-distance apart. Place your hands at your sides, just under the lowest ribs you can find. Position your hands so your thumbs come around your back and your fingers wrap around your front, with your index fingers positioned just under the lower ribs. Press in with your hands to create mild resistance, expanding your lower ribs against your hands. Take a full breath through your nose, filling your abdomen, middle, and then upper chest, concentrating on the expansion of the lower ribs.

⋛ The basic mechanics of deep diaphragmatic breathing include three parts: (1) inhale deeply through the nose for a count of five or so, making sure the abdomen rises and feeling the lower ribs expand against your hands; (2) hold the breath for three to five seconds; and (3) exhale completely through the mouth for a count longer than the inhalation. Once your lungs are empty and your belly is contracted, repeat the cycle. Complete eight to ten cycles.

Your goal is to breathe three dimensionally, expanding on all sides and aiming your breath toward your back as well as the front. This brings a feeling of being centered along the axis of your spine, and your attention will be drawn inward with the breath.

Tactical Breathing

Tactical breathing, also called combat breathing, is what helps firefighters race into burning buildings, police officers rush to the site of a crime, and soldiers fight in close combat. David Grossman, a lieutenant colonel in the elite US Army Rangers, helped to raise awareness of the benefits of tactical breathing, which helps first responders and military officers improve focus, gain control, and manage stress.

Why am I discussing this here? Few of us will face these types of high-risk, high-stress situations in everyday life. But tactical breathing is a technique to reassert control over your self-regulated sympathetic response (fight, flight, freeze), which you can experience anywhere—the board room, your boss's office, during a confrontation—not just on the battlefield. The best part is that no one has to know you are using tactical breathing! You can use this deep-breathing technique inconspicuously in the middle of any distressing situation.

The Power of
Deep Diaphragmatic Breathing

Is it worth ten minutes per day to focus on your breath? If you think you can't find time to practice deep breathing exercises regularly, take a deep resounding breath, then think again. Studies have shown that deep diaphragmatic breathing:

1. reduces risk factors for heart disease such as such as lowering bad cholesterol (LDL), raising good cholesterol (HDL), lowering blood pressure, and stabilizing blood sugar;

2. improves mood by elevating serotonin, a neurotransmitter that helps to maintain mood balance;

3. reduces stress by lowering cortisol, the primary stress hormone;

4. helps lower blood sugar and, therefore, the risk of diabetes;

5. helps reduce cravings for processed carbohydrates;

6. slows the aging process by increasing the secretion of human growth hormone;

7. reduces the acidity level of the body, making it more alkaline and, thus, reducing the risk for inflammation;

8. improves mental focus and concentration by increasing blood flow to the prefrontal cortex of the brain;

9. facilitates weight loss by balancing stress hormones with anabolic hormones; and

10. improves quality of sleep.

How to do it:

⋛ Tactical breathing by its very nature is done "on the fly"—you may be standing, sitting, or even lying down.

⋛ Breathe from your diaphragm. Your belly expands, moving out to make room for the air, as you breathe in, and it contracts as you breathe out. Some imagery may help. Think of your belly as a balloon filling with air as you breathe in and emptying smoothly, automatically, as you breathe out.

⋛ Inhale through your nose, deeply, expanding your belly for a count of four.

⋛ Hold that breath in for a count of four.

⋛ Slowly exhale through your mouth, completely, contracting your belly for a count of four.

⋛ Hold the empty breath for a count of four.

⋛ Repeat four to eight times until you feel your body relax.

The Long Exhale

This breathing sequence focuses on inhaling and exhaling and gradually increasing your exhalation until it is twice the length of your inhalation, which relaxes the nervous system. Try this practice anytime you're experiencing anxiety or before bedtime to support a restful night's sleep.

Tactical Breathing Works!

I stayed at the Charles Hotel in Cambridge, Massachusetts, on a frigid winter night before an important business meeting in November 2015. At 2 a.m. I woke, somewhat disoriented, to the sound of a fire alarm followed by police sirens—was there an emergency? All hotel guests were quickly evacuated, most wearing pajamas and overcoats. I quickly descended six flights of stairs in my bathrobe and slippers and found myself with the other shivering, half-dressed guests in the cold outside. I had a major presentation that day—I felt tense, cold, and agitated. The answer to my distress was tactical breathing. I began to use these techniques in the moment, and after four cycles of breath I could feel my body begin to relax. And—good news—false alarm! I trudged back to bed after sixty minutes and slept through the remainder of the night.

How to do it:

⋟ Sit in a chair in comfortable position, with your spine erect and your feet flat on the floor, about hip-distance apart. Place a palm on your abdomen, and take a few relaxed breaths through your nose only, feeling your abdomen expand on inhalation and gently contract on exhalation. Count the length of each inhalation and exhalation for several more breaths. If the inhalation is longer than the exhalation, begin to make them the same length over the next few breaths.

⋟ Once your inhalation and exhalation are equal, gradually increase the length of your exhalation by one to two seconds by gently contracting the abdomen. As long as you're breathing smoothly and without strain, continue to gradually increase the length of your exhalations by one to two seconds once every few breaths. Keep going until your exhalation is up to twice the length of your inhalation, but not beyond. For example, if your inhalation is comfortably five seconds, the length of the exhalation should be ten seconds, but not longer. The exhalation consists of a progressive relaxation.

⋛ Breathe using this one-to-two (inhale-to-exhale) technique for eight to ten complete breaths. You can bump up the impact by mentally saying "reeeelaaaax" as you exhale. Finish with six to eight natural, relaxed breaths.

Try This in Two Minutes

Take a comfortable, seated position, making sure your spine is straight. Gently close your eyes. Take a long, deep breath in through your nose, and exhale out of your nose, two to three counts longer than your inhalation. How do you feel? Lengthening your exhalation is the fastest way to calm the mind, soothe the nervous system, and balance emotions. The slower you breathe, the quieter your mind will become. It's easy to make excuses and claim we have "no time" to practice, but in truth it simply takes this sixty seconds to help yourself feel calmer and more focused and grounded. I encourage you to try it. An investment of a few seconds may lead to a different and more desirable outcome in a future situation.

Before I practiced pranayama my decision making was often reactive at critical times. I am a quick thinker and sometimes easily riled. Breath work has helped me stay in control and make better decisions.

One of my colleagues, Susan, who had been a peer, was recently promoted to a higher-level role and was now my boss. Despite my attempts to initiate an early phone conversation (we resided in different states and had different primary offices) there was over a month of silence between us following this transition. Finally, we had an initial meeting by phone. After I congratulated her on her new role, she quickly and unexpectedly gave me some negative feedback that I didn't agree with. This was not a good way to start our new relationship—at least in my view. I was not only taken aback but furious: Who does she think she is? And why is she giving me an unplanned performance review? Is she going to be this blunt and unthoughtful (and basically impossible to deal with) in her new leadership role?

I wanted to hang up before I said something that I might regret later, but instead I took a few deep breaths and quickly modulated my emotions. Simply taking the time to breathe helped me manage my sudden and unexpected surge of negative feelings. I was then able to speak from a place of calm and reflection, thanking Susan for the feedback and asking for her input on how to best improve the situation. (In truth she had offered me some positives, but my immediate reaction had been only on the negatives. Does this sound familiar?) We had a collegial conversation, and Susan and I have sustained a collaborative and productive working relationship ever since.

When you feel grounded it's much easier to take a step back in challenging situations to gain clarity and perspective. Adopting a breathing practice will help you manage stress in your life. How can you cultivate a healthy relationship with stress? A good way to do so is to schedule a regular ten-minute breath-awareness practice—make it a part of your daily routine. Maybe you start to incorporate the practice before you pour your morning coffee, or you can find a postlunch window when you can sit quietly and focus on your breath. You can even set a calendar reminder that pings you to make it feel just as important as your afternoon meetings. (I often make time for breath awareness while I am waiting for a meeting to start.)

If ten minutes is too much time, it's simple enough to close your eyes and take sixty-second conscious breathing breaks at random moments during your day.

Breathing is the essence of life. The practice of pranayama helps pacify the mind and soothe the emotions, even in your most agitated, turbulent state, allowing you to make prudent and objective decisions—an essential part of good leadership. Breathe into a balanced mind that is capable of processing issues at multiple levels and develop a more holistic perspective in deciding what is beneficial and appropriate for all stakeholders. You will become a breathtakingly better leader.

Self-Reflection

Take a moment to sit quietly and check in with your breath.

1. Observe your breath without the intention of changing it. Be aware if the breath is changing anyway. Just be aware.

2. Where do you feel your breathing? Is there a part of your body where your breath is more noticeable?

3. What is the quality of your breathing? Is it smooth or rough, easy or labored, jerky or rhythmic, deep or shallow?

4. What is the pace of your breathing? Fast or slow?

5. Now gently close your eyes and breathe deeply and slowly, in and out through your nose, for a few minutes. Do you feel a release from tension, pain, or stress? What has shifted for you?

5

Freeing Yourself from Distraction

"[We are] distracted from distraction by distraction."
—T. S. Eliot, *Four Quartets*

Ten members of the senior leadership team sat at the table when I walked into a management meeting; all but two had their smartphones face up on the table, and every single one had left their laptop open. Most were composing and answering emails just prior to the beginning of the meeting. There was little conversation in the room. This is a typical image, indicative of the situation prior to and during most meetings.

For each of the five important topics on the agenda the presenters delivered with clarity and commitment—clearly my colleagues had worked steadfastly to bring forward their best work. Meanwhile most members of the leadership team were multitasking, reviewing, and sending email messages during the presentations, looking up occasionally to come up for air before diving back into the digital flow.

Business as usual.

Distractions in our corporate environment disperse one of our most important leadership assets: our attention. How much could those decision makers truly absorb with their eyes bouncing between tiny screens? How did the presenters feel when, after tireless work and a sleepless night, their carefully researched and crafted presentations met with such an obvious lack of engagement? Would they aim quite so high the next time they were expected to present?

Think about the last meeting you attended: How many of the attendees brought with them their laptop, cell phone, or both? How many of them gave their attention to other work during the meeting?

Sure, urgent business-related messages usually deserve a prompt response, but is it really necessary to respond to any and all incoming texts and emails the moment they arrive? Or have we all simply been conditioned to respond to a flashing notification icon no matter where we are or what else we may be doing? Many of us are hostage to our phones. As soon as we get that text or email alert, we check it and answer. It becomes a conditioned response.

And we engage in such behaviors not only at the office but also when we are not at work. Essentially we make ourselves available 24/7. Think about it. We constantly take out our phones to text or email. We are on our phones during meals. We interrupt our own conversations by taking out our phones. We sleep with our phones next to or under our pillows. Some of us even text while we drive, knowing that this activity is both dangerous and, in most places, illegal. We are evolving into a society that cannot wait. It does not matter how high the stakes are or if we have well-understood warnings. Our love of our smartphones encroaches on our personal time and our relationships and may even be dangerous to others. (By the way, do you feel a need to check your phone now? Something might be happening that requires your immediate attention, or that urge to look for a new notification may simply be a compulsion you don't need to indulge.)

If you're like me, you feel bombarded by information. But some of this overload we actually bring on ourselves. I was recently visiting my second home in Sanibel Island, Florida. I have been traveling to Sanibel at least once a year since I was a small child, and I cherish my time on this peaceful island. Sanibel is an East-West barrier island that has vast sandy beaches with an abundance of shells. It's a great place to vacation—or to live—and to enjoy shelling, fishing, and bird watching. For me it's a great place to tap into my creativity and to write. Sound idyllic? It is. Although I make a conscious effort during my time on Sanibel to keep my phone put away—at least most of the time—in recent years I have been astounded by the number of people on the beach with their phones out, talking or texting. They are missing the beauty of their natural surroundings. Rather than hearing the chirping of the birds, they attend to the chirping of their phones. They miss the experience of life unfolding—the wonders of nature, the serenity of the ocean, and the beauty of their surroundings.

The Information Overload Research Group—a group of industry practitioners, academic researchers, and other professionals—is dedicated to addressing the problem of information overload. Jonathan Spira, one of the group's founders and author of *Overload!: How Too Much Information Is Hazardous to Your Organization*, states, "Overload causes people to lose their ability to manage thoughts and ideas, contemplate, and even reason and think. It has resulted in work days that never seem to end, completely destroying work/life balance."

Of course, our cell phones are just one factor in our busy and overstimulated lives. The next time you take a reading break, look around you. Are you surrounded by computer screens, televisions, or other display devices? Are other people having conversations? Can you hear the traffic going by? Our world is noisy and full of people and things competing for our attention.

So how can we deal with the continuous stimulation and information overload? You've got it—yoga! As the fifth of the eight limbs of yoga, *pratyahara* occupies a central place. It is not possible to move directly from asana practice to meditation, from the body to the mind, without attention to what lies in between. To make this transition we must bring our energies, our impulses, and our senses—the components that link body and mind—into alignment. With pranayama we rein in our energies and impulses (see Chapter 4); with pratyahara we gain mastery over the unruly senses.

The term *pratyahara* is composed of two Sanskrit words: *prati* and *ahara*. Ahara means food, or anything we take into ourselves from the outside. Prati means away or against. Thus, pratyahara literally means to push against external influences, to withdraw the mind from the world of external objects. It is the yogic practice of turning the mind inward, voluntarily shutting out the distractions provided by the senses. We still register the input from our eyes and ears, but we don't *react* to that input.

For many yoga students the practice of pratyahara can be elusive. The relentless onslaught of sensory input seems as unavoidable as water in a raging thunderstorm, but pratyahara rests upon the principle that we do in fact have the capability to influence our response to that input.

Through the practice of pratyahara we learn to create a gap between the world around us and our response to that world. This gap gives us the necessary space to choose the best response—instead of simply reacting. Despite our best intentions, we cannot entirely avoid the never-ending stimuli of modern society. But we can learn to remain poised and present in the middle of all the noise and interruptions.

Pratyahara is a path to effective leadership, exemplified by:

› Identifying and acting on true priorities

› Exhibiting openness

› Being grounded

› Directly communicating

› Giving others your full attention

› Choosing your responses rather than having knee-jerk reactions

We tend to see stimulation as a necessity or as an escape. Personally, I know how difficult it can be to step away from distractions. I try to attend a master-level yoga class a few times per month. The class meets over the lunch hour during the work week. On many occasions I have arrived about ten minutes early, put my mat near a wall, and taken my computer and phone into the room with me to finish my emails and text messages *immediately* prior to the start of class. (Of course, this is strictly prohibited, but I justify my behavior knowing that I have shown up during my busy day and prioritized my practice.) But—here's a question I ask myself, fearful of the answer: Is what I am doing really necessary? I always more than make up the time I spend in class, and there are rarely urgent matters in those few minutes that require my attention. Nevertheless, I repeat the behavior at the risk of my teacher noticing and kicking me out of class. Think about your own experiences, whether in a meeting, at a class, or while spending time with family and friends. What things do you allow to intrude on your time and divide your focus?

Distractions decrease focus, of course, but they also increase stress—despite the immediate sense of relief we feel when we allow ourselves to check our social media notifications in the middle of a tedious task. Leaders who learn to rely on distraction to escape from important challenges become myopic, often putting their energy into trivial activities that deliver little value and sap their creativity and commitment to a larger mission. They respond to an "urgent" but unimportant email instead of rethinking their strategy for the next quarter. Where is their attention most sorely needed?

Believe me: I know firsthand that external distractions are hard to avoid. At the office there are constant interruptions: audible email alerts, coworkers stopping by, phone calls, text messages, or other people's conversations, especially if you work in an open setting, just to name a few. And if you work at home you're faced with a different set of things clamoring for your attention: the doorbell, half-completed chores, possibly even children to look after. Regardless of our location, we are often "running" all day among various meetings, projects, committees, initiatives, and so on. It's not practical or easy to completely shut down if your job or the needs of your family require you to be in constant contact or you're expecting important incoming messages.

Here are nine ways to manage the need to stay connected and still have a chance to unplug:

Establish boundaries. Reserve regular blocks of time for work that requires intense concentration. Ask your coworkers for quiet time by putting a polite "Please do not disturb: on tight deadline" sign on your door or outside your office cubicle. And keep yourself in check by turning off email notifications and silencing your phone. If you work in an open office and are distracted—and less productive—due to the conversations of those around you, consider using headphones at your desk. They can be a helpful auditory boundary between you and other noise in the office. Just make sure that whatever music or sound you choose isn't creating another distraction. I personally prefer to work in silence but sometimes find ambient noise soothing, such as the sounds of ocean waves or rainfall.

Listen actively. Active listening is a technique in which you restate, in your own words, what you've heard back to the person who's speaking. This helps you stay engaged with the speaker and avoid getting distracted or losing focus. The ability to listen actively demonstrates sincerity and helps to ensure that the speaker knows he is not being taken for granted. Try it a few times and notice the difference in your conversations and how others perceive you.

Take short breaks throughout the day. Allow yourself to rest and regain energy by stepping away from your work or the task at hand. Ideally the best place to do this is to take a walk outside. But if that's not possible, gaze outside through a window. A University of Melbourne study found that the simple act of glancing at a grassy green roof for only forty seconds markedly increased participants' concentration. Even taking minibreaks, as short as thirty seconds, throughout the day can help you regain focus.

Turn off all nonessential notifications. You may need to hear when an email arrives in your inbox (though maybe not—email is such a big factor in office distractions that I devote more attention to it below).

But do you really need an alert every time your family or friends post something on Facebook or regular interruptions from your news apps? By changing your notifications settings to allow only the most critical information to filter through, you'll feel more relaxed knowing you're not jumping every time your phone or computer pings.

Clear your home screen. Is your home screen cluttered? Chances are you've downloaded many apps that seemed useful in the moment. But now you no longer use them, although they still appear on your home screen. Organize your apps by keeping only the most essential ones visible when you first turn on your phone, and move everything else to the next screen. You can also organize your apps by sorting them into folders like "Social Media," "Travel," "Fitness," and so on so you'll be able to find them easily.

Keep a technology basket handy. If you're seeking more quality time in your office or at home, designate a basket or box as the "tech holder" and leave your phone there instead of out on your desk or in your purse or pocket. You'll likely still hear when important messages come through, but you won't be as tempted to reach for your phone every five seconds. This is a great tool to encourage others to stay focused too, whether it's during a meeting or a family dinner. It could be the best hour or two of your day!

Check your devices on a regular basis, not as messages come in. A recent study indicated that some mobile device owners check their devices eighty-five times per day, accounting for about one-third of waking hours! Many people check their phones first thing in the morning and the last thing that they do at night—and sometimes even in the middle of the night!

Control instant messaging (IM). Many workplaces use an IM platform to keep team members in touch with one another. However, it can be a source of distraction, a steady stream of conversations, nonessential notifications, and emojis. Personally, I find IM to be a major obstruction to keeping focused throughout my day, so I don't use it much. But if you must IM, get into the habit of using it for quick exchanges only, not for long conversations. Resist replying instantly, and consider setting specific times during the day when your status is "available."

The quintessential challenge. Try to go a whole day without your mobile phone. If you fear what will happen if others are unable to reach you, let them know beforehand that they need to contact you through other means or wait until you've taken your phone again. At the end of the day consider: How did that feel? Any withdrawal symptoms? Any positive reactions by the end of the day? Of course, this just isn't realistic for most of us to do every day, but perhaps you'll find that you don't need to be *always* reachable and will feel more comfortable leaving your phone in your desk when you go out to lunch, attend a meeting, or are spending quality time with others.

I've started scheduling "distraction" and "nondistraction" hours. I answer emails and am available on the IM platform at my office at scheduled times during the day (which vary depending upon the business need). I ask my colleagues to call my mobile phone if they have an urgent matter that immediately requires my attention. Practiced regularly, pratyahara is a powerful tool that supports our intention to be consciously present for every moment of our lives.

For most of us emails are a constant, regular part of our workday and have become a primary mode of communication. It's often easier to send a quick email than it is to pick up the phone or walk to a nearby

Reflect and Build Capacity

Take time—even just a few minutes—to reflect at the end your day. Remembering specific instances when you successfully navigated calm moments amidst the storm of a hectic day can help you implement them again. Ask yourself: How much time did you spend doing things in ways that helped you achieve your most important goals? When did you feel the most productive, and what did your environment look like? What tweaks really made a difference in the way you got things done? Consider writing these down and keeping these strategies around your workspace so you have a constant reminder of ways to successfully avoid distraction and be more productive.

office, even if it's next door. But in reality many of the emails that ping in our inboxes are not particularly important or even necessary. Although email is an essential communication and work tool, it is also a threat to efficiency and productivity. How many emails have you received in the past week that contained nonessential information? We're bombarded with emails, and we tend to look at them the second that they arrive, regardless of what the subject says or what else we're doing at the time (I know I'm guilty of glancing at my email too often and wherever I might be!).

Here are five ways to better manage your emails so they do not lead to constant distraction and disruption.

Schedule set time(s) to check your email. Don't let emails build up until they become totally unmanageable, but also don't feel the need to have your email open constantly, pulling you away from other tasks that require your attention. (I promise you that most matters can wait!) Check and respond to messages at set times during the day—perhaps first thing in the morning, before lunch, and near the end of your day. Manage your colleagues' and customers' expectations as to how and when you will reply to them by letting them know when to expect a response; for example, set up an auto-reply message that says when you check your messages and that you will try to respond within twenty-four hours. This gives you the space to handle your inbox on your own time without feeling overwhelmed and pressured to answer everything all at once.

Try using the "two-minute rule." This is a terrific tip I have borrowed from David Allen, author of *Getting Things Done*. When you read your email, if the email will take less than two minutes to read and reply to, take care of it immediately. The idea behind this is that if it takes less than two minutes to take action, it takes longer to read and then store the task away "to do later" than it would to just take care of it now. For emails that will take longer than two minutes, file them in visible "To Do" folders that denote the urgency and complexity, then take care of them during the time you've set aside to handle these longer tasks.

Set up an email filing system. Creating specific folders for processing email makes it easier to search for and retrieve past email (see the above "To Do" folder, or maybe you file emails per project or client). While maintaining an "inbox zero," or completely empty inbox, is unrealistic for most of us, a filing system that you use regularly will help keep your inbox from getting out of control, eliminating that source of stress and supporting a more organized approach.

Write clear and succinct emails. Keep your messages short and to the point, and remember that anything you send out electronically is out there forever! It's always wise to maintain a professional, even formal tone at work, setting a good example for colleagues and clients. Also, don't overcommunicate. One of my pet peeves is overuse of the Reply All function—for example, I often receive emails that say, "Thank you" that are intended for someone else on the chain. It's nice to know that good manners are alive and well, but I'd rather have one less email to open! (This leads to my next point . . .)

Use the trash. Delete irrelevant emails immediately! Don't be afraid to get rid of emails once you've handled the contents. Letting emails pile up in your inbox is like letting piles of laundry accumulate around the house—pretty soon you can't see the couch anymore and you have nothing to wear! Don't lose sight of what's important in your inbox. Once you have replied to an email, file it or trash it.

I value working with cross-cultural teams and especially working with colleagues in Japan. It is imperative that I understand Japanese business practices in order to effectively collaborate and ultimately foster a unified voice. When I first traveled to Japan I was struck by my colleagues' silence after I would speak about a challenging or controversial topic. Were they bored? Disengaged? I thought I was a passionate speaker!

I later learned that in times of stress or difficulty during a meeting the Japanese often resort to silence in order to release the tension in the room and allow people to move away from the area of difficulty—to preserve harmony, which is tantamount. So I now resist the urge to fill the silence with more talk that Japanese team members prefer to avoid in the moment. My yoga practice has helped me embrace silence,

French Law Bars
Work Email after Hours

In France a law establishing workers' "right to disconnect" went into effect on January 1, 2017. Companies with more than fifty employees are now required to establish hours when employees should not send or answer emails. According to the French Ministry of Labor the law was designed "to ensure respect for rest periods and . . . balance between work and family and personal life."

Of course, I understand that after-hours email is not a bad thing in itself. In a recent survey Gallup found that more than 75 percent of full-time workers thought the ability to use their work cell phones, computers, and other mobile technology outside of normal working hours is a "somewhat positive" or "strongly positive" development. It may allow you to be more flexible with demands on your time during the nine-to-five time frame.

Still, occasionally checking in on work matters after hours is not the same as being available to your colleagues 24/7. At a certain point are you allowing email to intrude on time you could be spending with loved ones, at the gym or yoga studio, or while recharging your batteries a bit? So it's time to consider: If a country has implemented such radical action, is it time for you to do the same to counter your own email overload? What can you learn from France's example?

allowing me to be more aware of my impulses and reactions. Through this awareness I am less likely to act in ways I may regret later, as I recognize that Japanese people highly value silence as a fundamental form of nonverbal communication. We tend to view silence in the Western world as the mere absence of speech or sound, but in reality silence can be a powerful tool of communication.

One of the most common practices for pratyahara is to practice pranayama, or deep breathing techniques. As little as one deep, full breath drawn from the belly can help stop mental chatter and intrusive thoughts (see also Chapter 4).

The STOP technique is commonly used to help you to remember the process:

- **S**top what you are doing; put things down for a minute.

- **T**ake a few deep breaths.

- **O**bserve your experience just as it is, including thoughts, feelings, and emotions.

- **P**roceed with something that will support you in the moment, such as talking to a colleague or friend or walking outdoors for a short period.

This practice gives you time to recenter. Once you have established that space between you and your surroundings, you can act more intentionally, making decisions from a nonreactive place.

As a leader you must maintain an active and continuing state of self-reflection, with a focus on understanding and evaluating your personal values and whether your actions, moment by moment, match those values.

The Value of Silence

Most of us don't like silence. We fear the feelings of emptiness and insignificance as well as a loss of relevance. We crave being seen in the eyes of another, yet in silence we must confront ourselves.

The practice of pratyahara supports the need to minimize distractions and focus attention, allowing for conscious, nonreactive decision making. A quick way to practice pratyahara is to turn off Facebook, email notifications, Twitter, your phone, and any other electronic devices and then sit for five minutes in silence. Being in silence helps us connect with ourselves and learn to connect with others by remaining still and being present. Silence helps bring us back to a place of peace and clarity within, away from the noise in our world. Protect this space in your daily schedule; it won't just happen in our society riddled with distractions.

Inquiry—asking questions—is at the heart of this reflection. Asking yourself questions about your actions, your impact, and your influence on others builds emotional intelligence, which is acknowledged to be one of the most important and underdeveloped skills in the business world today. Warren Buffett, CEO of Berkshire Hathaway, is the most successful investor of the twentieth century. He has stated that success in investing doesn't correlate with IQ: "Once you have ordinary intelligence, what you need is the temperament to control the urges that get other people into trouble investing." The practice of pratyahara can help you modulate temperament.

I travel regularly to Massachusetts to study yoga. On a recent drive there from my home in Connecticut, I received an emergency weather alert on my iPhone: a tornado warning for the area. (Yes, this is one notification that is worth leaving on your devices!) It was a bright, sunny afternoon, so I ignored the message.

At four in the afternoon I was scheduled for a coveted private yoga lesson with my teacher, something I had been looking forward to for some time. I arrived at her home studio a few minutes early and parked my car on the street in front of her home. Shortly after I settled onto my mat a rumble of thunder shivered through the polished wood floor of her third-floor studio. An eye-blink later the skies opened up, and a torrential rainstorm swept the area, accompanied by lightning, thunder, and, most troublingly, hail the size of golf balls.

In the past I would have spent the following thirty minutes of nature's fury entirely absent from the lesson for which I had waited so patiently, going through the motions while simmering in anger at the fact that my new car was parked outside in a hailstorm. Focused on the imagined damage to my vehicle, the presumed dents, and the hypothetical repair bill, I would have compounded the unfortunate situation by missing out on an incredible learning opportunity.

Instead, through the practice of pratyahara, I detached myself from the world outside. Clearly, we were safe inside, and whatever happened to my car would simply happen. No amount of worry, frustration, or rage would prevent a single ding from appearing on that glossy gray hood.

Thankfully I stayed present for my lesson. When I emerged outside refreshed and glowing (to a sunny-once-more afternoon), I saw that my car had—big surprise—sustained significant hail damage. At that moment, however, I felt nothing but gratitude at the fact that both my teacher and I were unharmed. After all, my car could be repaired or—if need be—replaced.

Practicing Pratyahara at a Practical, Everyday Level

I suggest practicing pratyahara daily for at least ten minutes in order to develop some measure of mastery over the senses. (If you are saying to yourself, *I can't take that much time out of my busy day*, remember that one day has 1,440 minutes, so can you spare ten of those?)

- Turn off all electronics and sit in silence for a few minutes, paying attention to your breath and how you are feeling.

- Sitting with your eyes closed, focus on your breath. When you breathe out, at the end of the exhale try to breathe out a little bit more, even if you feel your lungs are empty. This is a way to eliminate toxicity of both mind and matter.

- Eat one meal a day in silence—not in front of the TV or computer—tasting and experiencing every bite.

- Clear the physical clutter around you. A clean and organized environment can help with "mental tidying" and improve your internal focus.

- Close your eyes, eliminating outside distractions, and focus inward for thirty seconds several times per day.

- Take a walk in nature and become aware of the sounds around you, focusing on those that are most subtle and difficult to hear.

- Practice self-reflection by journaling for a few minutes every day.

- Prior to going to sleep at night, try to shut down your senses one at a time—sight, hearing, smell, taste, touch. Your sleep should be more restful.

So next time you are in your office, listening to music in the background while engaged on the phone in a teleconference, your eyes glued to your computer screen as email messages come in—take a pause. Practiced regularly, pratyahara is a powerful tool that supports our intention to be consciously present for every moment of our lives. And practicing pratyahara could even save lives in critical situations. On January 15, 2009, Captain Chesley "Sully" Sullenberger safely landed a US Airways airbus in the Hudson River after Canadian geese knocked out both engines. To safely glide the plane into the Hudson, Sullenberger had to shed distractions, including his own fear of death. He made the right decision about where to land; his performance required extraordinary concentration. Six months later, as reported in *Fly by Wire: The Geese, the Glide, the Miracle on the Hudson* by William Langewiesche, Sullenberger summarized his actions at the National Transportation Safety Board hearing in Washington, DC: "I think it is that paying attention matters. That having awareness constantly matters. Continuing to build that mental model to build a team matters." Sullenberger was able to rein in his mind and saved the lives of the 155 people on board.

Self-Reflection

1. Do you suffer from sensory overload?

2. Are you easily distracted?

3. How many hours per day do you spend in front of screens?

4. Is your productivity compromised by distractions?

5. How do you feel when you take a break from technology?

6. Can you put your mobile phone on "silent" without upset or agitation for two hours? Eight hours? A full day? What are the benefits to you when you do so?

7. How do you stop yourself from reacting to challenging situations?

8. Can you sit in silence for five minutes? What comes up in your mind during those five minutes?

6

Becoming Present to
the Challenge

"Concentrate all your thoughts upon the work at hand.
The sun's rays do not burn until brought to a focus."
—Alexander Graham Bell

Do you multitask in order to achieve more faster? I did too before I realized that multitasking is actually a myth.

Not too long ago my team was waiting for some key information from the US Food and Drug Administration that would influence the design of a pivotal clinical trial. We'd waited a long time for their assessment, and when it finally came through, I circulated a document and called a meeting to discuss the information. Most team members were scattered throughout the United States and Europe, so I set up a teleconference. As we discussed these critical materials from our locations in various places throughout the world I heard a cacophony of sounds in the background: someone tapping on a keyboard, a baby crying, a doorbell ringing, cars honking, the shuffling of papers, and more. Was anyone listening? How much of this important information was anyone hearing, much less absorbing and understanding? Was anyone fully engaged in the conversation?

Doing one thing at a time is no longer enough. Most of us practice multitasking, and it is ingrained in our daily lives. As you read this chapter, are you also attending to a text message, composing an email, checking Facebook, or talking on the phone? Be honest! Do you know that the constant interruption and distraction that comes from multitasking disrupts our ability to stay focused and present? Don't think this is a big deal? Over time it puts you at a disadvantage when working on important projects, juggling your job and family, or simply staying engaged with whatever you are doing in the present.

Web surfing has been termed "the new secondhand smoke." Even sitting next to someone multitasking on a laptop could affect your learning and performance, according to a 2012 Canadian study. Not only did students who multitasked during class have reduced comprehension of lecture material, those in view of multitaskers also had reduced comprehension.

The belief that engaging in several tasks at once means we are more productive is a myth. In recent years researchers have proven that multitasking—extolled for years as a key trait of high achievers (and practiced by many, if not most, in corporate settings)—was a myth. Medical research reveals that the brain does not really do tasks simultaneously. Further, if we do too many things at once, our brains lose the capacity for deep thinking altogether. When we divide our attention among tasks what we're really doing is "task switching"—that is, focusing for a brief period on one task, then another, then another. In each moment we only focus long enough to feel (and look) busy but never enough to truly engage with the problem and develop a novel and effective solution to it. Our attention is expended by switching tasks instead of on becoming fully engaged with any single activity.

Rather than saving time, multitasking actually costs us time, and it also makes mistakes more likely. As we rapidly switch contexts, we actually *lose* focus, and it may take longer to become re-engaged in a single task and achieve a deep level of thought. This is not a recipe for success.

The last chapter dealt with pratyahara, the practice of putting a boundary between yourself and the many external stimuli vying for your attention during your waking hours. Now we will see the other side of that coin: not just freeing yourself from distraction but also learning to focus your attention with precision and intent.

Dharana means focus, concentrating fully on the task in front of you, whether that task is finishing a report, answering an email, or playing make-believe with your child. That feeling when your mind is simultaneously still and active, when you are completely engrossed in a complex challenge or an exciting conversation, when you are "firing on all cylinders"—this is dharana. However, dharana isn't just about getting your work done more effectively; it's a discipline for enjoying life's pleasures and challenges with the same undistracted sense of presence, living each of life's moments to its fullest.

As we'll discuss further in Chapter 8, noted psychologist Mihaly Csikszentmihalyi calls this state *flow*. Flow, also known as *the zone*, is a state of concentration or complete absorption with the situation and activity at hand. The flow state is an optimal state of intrinsic motivation with a feeling of an energized focus. It's when we're fully immersed in what we're doing. Csikszentmihalyi has done a great deal of research into how flow works, how it differs from our typical experience, and why it's so important. But understanding intellectually what flow—or dharana—is and actually being able to experience it on demand are two entirely different things. We commonly hear "live in the moment," but what does that actually look and feel like?

Some people spend their lives focusing on the past, comfortable with the status quo and wishing things weren't changing. Others are future orientated—dreaming, wishing, and planning for "that next best thing." Their present typically fades to gray, and they fail to enjoy the moment because they are already striving for the next goal.

A primary task of leadership is to capture and direct the collective attention of a group or a team. To do this well, leaders must learn to focus their own attention. In his book *Focus: The Hidden Ingredient in Excellence*, Daniel Goleman explains why leaders need to cultivate a three-part system of awareness—an inward focus, a focus on others, and an outward focus. The inward focus (self) refers to self-awareness, our capacity to identify thoughts, feelings, and bodily sensations occurring within us, as well as self-management, how we manage ourselves, which includes regulating our emotions and resulting behaviors. The focus on others (people) means empathy, or how well we attune to people, which allows us to understand another person's condition from their perspective. Some people see empathy as a weakness, but it's not. Successful leaders focus on supporting and enabling others, and being empathic helps them better collaborate, motivate others, and serve as a positive influence. Finally, the outward focus (systems) has to do with how well we can focus on the wider world and the forces that shape it, such as organizational dynamics, innovative technologies, and political trends. A strong outer focus allows leaders to develop a winning strategy that anticipates change before it occurs.

In an effort to focus my own work I wrote a portion of this book in the quiet town of Woodstock, Vermont. I first stumbled across

Try This in Two Minutes

Keep a daily journal. If you are not accustomed to journaling, start with only two minutes per day. Sound doable? Focus your writing on the range of feelings you've had throughout your day: How did your feelings influence your actions? If you cannot recognize your feelings, you can't control them. Writing your thoughts down gives you an opportunity to explore and reflect on what you truly think and feel. When you are honest about your thoughts and feelings, you learn to be more authentic with yourself. Look back at your writing every now and then to see what themes you have covered. This is a good way to better understand your underlying thoughts and belief systems.

Woodstock while attending a yoga retreat in nearby Plymouth. I had taken a short drive to explore the local area and stopped in this quintessential northeast village in the heart of the Green Mountains. There I found a wonderful haven for creative thinking and writing, an authentic and peaceful place where I could quiet my mind, focus my attention, gel my ideas, and put words on a page with a sense of freedom and contentment. My home in Connecticut is typically filled with distractions, so on four occasions I journeyed the 190 miles to my writing sanctuary. The peaceful environment in Woodstock allowed me to be in the moment, and my writing flowed.

We'd all like to be more focused, self-motivated, and capable of achieving high levels of productivity without getting mired in the myth of multitasking—and elements of yoga can help us get there.

Emotional Focus

A keen awareness and regulation of our emotions is central to the productive use of our attention. Psychologist Susan David has studied emotions, happiness, and achievement for more than twenty years, and she has found that no matter how intelligent or creative people are or what type of personality they have, it's how they navigate their inner world—their thoughts, feelings, and self-talk—that ultimately determines how successful they will become. The way we respond to our internal experiences not only drives our actions but also impacts our relationships, happiness, and health. Emotionally agile people experience stress and setbacks, as we all do, but they are able to adapt and regulate their emotions. They put their best selves forward by approaching their inner experiences in a mindful, values-driven, and productive way.

A decade ago almost no one had a smartphone. Now, many of us reach for our phones the second we wake up in the morning. We fear missing out on something important or urgent—and let's be honest, how many emails are mislabeled "urgent?"—so we constantly check our phones and our email. A recent study showed that we touch our phones an average or 2,617 times per day! Most of us don't even realize how often we check our phones, demonstrating that some of our mobile phone interactions are habitual.

What you also may not realize is that many of us actually hold our breath while concentrating on our screens. Linda Stone coined the term *email apnea*—a habit of shallow breathing or holding our breath while managing emails—and 80 percent of us suffer from it, according to the *Huffington Post*. Take a moment and think about the last time you checked your email: Were you consciously computing, or do you have email apnea?

So how can we use dharana to focus our attention and manage the constant onslaught of emails, text messages, phone calls, and the pull of social media? It should come as no surprise by now that a regular yoga practice—including breathing techniques, poses, and meditation—helps with focus by calming the mind and minimizing distractions. In Yoga Sutra 1.2 (the second chapter of book one), Patanjali explains the definition and purpose of yoga, "*yoga chitta vritti nirodha*," which can be translated from Sanskrit to English as "yoga is the reduction of the fluctuations of the mind."

Well, that sounds great, but how does it work? I ask you to consider a practical—and quick—approach, one that even those who claim "I have no time!" can fit into a busy schedule. Breath awareness is a fundamental part of every yoga practice. Three to five minutes of nadi shodhana pranayma (alternate nostril breathing) will help you reach a calm, clear, and focused state of mind. Nadi shodhana pranayama is particularly effective because it fosters calm and mental clarity and brings balance to the right and left hemispheres of the brain. I often practice this breathing exercise before a big presentation or an important meeting, as it not only allows me to focus clearly on the task at hand but also relaxes me and helps calm any anxieties I might have.

As you practice alternate nostril breathing, notice the quality of the breath: the temperature, speed, and strength as well as how your nostrils expand or contract when you breathe and any other sensations that arise. Your mind may wander, but keep bringing your attention back to your breathing, and let any distractions pass. It's a simple activity that offers incredibly profound benefits.

Try This in Two Minutes

Alternate nostril breathing: start by finding a relaxed, comfortable, seated position, with your spine erect and chin level to the ground. Begin by closing your eyes and taking a deep breath in and out through your nose. Then press your right thumb against your right nostril, and inhale slowly and steadily through your left nostril. At the end of your inhalation close off the left nostril with your ring finger so both nostrils are briefly held closed, then release your thumb and exhale slowly through your right nostril. Continue with an alternating pattern. With your ring finger pressing against your left nostril, inhale slowly through your right nostril, close it off with your right thumb, pause, and then exhale through your left nostril. Practice for at least two minutes, and then allow your breath to return to normal, noticing any change you might feel. Alternate nostril breathing boosts parasympathetic modulation and has been shown to improve attention, among other benefits.

In addition to breathing, meditation is one of the best ways to train your brain to stay on task. We'll try one short meditation now and discuss this topic in more depth in Chapter 7. A meditative exercise that is particularly effective in finding stillness in the mind is to focus on the small pauses that naturally occur at the end of each inhalation and at the end of each exhalation during breathing cycles. Awareness of these pauses is a very simple and efficient method for quieting and clearing the mind.

We all face intense demands on our time and often find ourselves booked nonstop for days on end. I recently traveled to five

Try This in Two Minutes

Start by finding a relaxed, comfortable, seated position, with your spine erect and chin level to the ground. Gently close your eyes. Take a few moments to "simply be." Notice whatever is being experienced in the moment—sounds, physical sensations, thoughts, feelings—without trying to do anything about it.

Bring your attention to the breath. Simply notice the breath as it moves in and out. Now become aware of the point at which the breath turns the corner from the inhalation to the exhalation and from the exhalation to the inhalation. As you continue practicing this meditation, you may find that the stillness is no longer experienced as discrete gaps between the breaths but rather is a more continuous experience. This cultivates the awareness of stillness in the midst of activity and can create a profound experience of peace.

European countries in a three-week period to deliver three high-stakes presentations to regulatory authorities. It was exhausting! However, I built time into each day for exercise, yoga, and brief breaks outdoors to enjoy nature or some sightseeing, even just an hour or two each day. This space for myself gave me the breathing room—literally—to adjust to different time zones, rest and re-energize, and stay focused.

You can expand your attentive capacity through regular practices such as alternate nostril breathing, which you learned in this chapter, meditation (which we will explore in more depth in Chapter 7), journaling, spending time outdoors, physical activity, healthy and regular eating, and getting plenty of sleep. I strive to follow all these practices on a routine basis and find that I am much more efficient and effective when I do. However, things are never perfect, and I don't beat myself up when I can't do it all. Sleep is the biggest problem for me. I know that good-quality sleep supports creativity, productivity, and engagement at work. My sleep is often erratic due to travel and insufficient due to the overall demands on my time. I often work on my computer until just before I go to bed—bad idea!. How about you? Have you ever found yourself lying awake at night staring at your phone? Many of us grab our phones after lights out. Or we might read an e-book in bed. Exposure to screens, particularly around bedtime, may have a negative impact on sleep. Why? The light from our devices is "short-wavelength enriched," meaning it has a higher concentration of blue light than natural light. Blue light affects levels of the sleep-inducing hormone melatonin more than any other wavelength. Increased screen time may lead to poor sleep, and poor sleep may lead to increased screen time. It can be a vicious cycle. So all we can do is be aware of the benefits of sticking to the practices outlined in this book, and try to achieve them as often as possible. None of us is perfect.

Our most precious resource is time. But even in an endless time-frame, without the ability to focus, it's tough to get the job done. Minimizing distractions and directing our attention on specific tasks or interactions—practicing dharana—greatly improves our impact at work and in life.

Leadership begins when you are fully present. Being present is being in and holding a centered position with open access to both mind and body. It means being open to and in touch with your own authentic feelings as well as those of others.

Personal presence is about being present in the moment, bringing your highest energy and best self forward, and being truly authentic.

Schedule a Break at Work

Do you think you are too busy for a break?

What if taking a break would allow you to do your job more effectively?

It is important to open some space in your calendar on a daily basis to find time to focus on people and things you enjoy beyond the scope of work. Finding such space allows for more creative thinking and helps replenish our stores of attention while at work. Indeed, studies have found that those who allow themselves a brief distraction once an hour while working perform better at their task than those who keep hammering away without allowing themselves a break. Investing in yourself is not an indulgence! Can you spare thirty minutes for yourself in a 480-minute (eight-hour) workday? Try to schedule ten minutes three times per day. It could be as simple as getting up to get yourself a glass of water or make a cup of tea. If you have time to schedule a longer break or want to make full use of your lunch hour, you might even find a nearby gym or yoga studio. Add these breaks to your calendar, and commit to taking them. Reflect after one week: Are you are actually more focused, productive, and in a better mood? You deserve a hard-earned break.

People with personal presence are confident and speak clearly and persuasively. They think clearly, even under pressure, and they act with intention. They reflect on their emotions, attitudes, and situations and are able to adapt. They accept responsibility for themselves and the results they achieve—whether positive or negative.

The perception of "personal presence" dictates decisions and actions. For example, managers with strong personal presence often persuade the best people to join their team. Organizations and nations tend to elect their leaders based on the power of personal presence as conveyed through the media. Former president Barack Obama has strong personal presence. His keynote address at the 2004 Democratic National Convention instantly earned the then senator a reputation as a great orator and helped him rise quickly within the Democratic Party. Angela Merkel, chancellor of Germany since 2005 and the first-ever female German chancellor, has transformed German politics and topped the *Forbes* list of the world's most powerful women in 2016. Merkel is known for her down-to-earth style and strong self-confidence.

Personal presence is a state of being, and when mastered, it can allow you to tap into your values, put them into action, and act decisively. People with strong personal presence influence and inspire those around them.

A challenge for most leaders is to be focused and present, determine what needs to be done, and facilitate making that happen. Not only do effective leaders focus on results; they also find importance, value, meaning, and enjoyment in their work. Noted author Simon Sinek believes that great leaders ask themselves: Why? In his book *Start with Why, How Great Leaders Inspire Everyone to Take Action*, Sinek says, "People don't buy what you do; they buy why you do it. And what you do simply proves what you believe."

My *why* behind writing this book is that I found the principles and practice of yoga to be transformative in my own life and wanted to share my learnings. Although this book focuses on a model for leadership, the ideas and concepts have a broader context in our modern era. This context transcends leadership and supports global health and wellness initiatives. How? We live in a world of excessive noise and social media. Social media is addictive. We often find ourselves logging into Facebook, YouTube, Twitter, LinkedIn, and more, often simultaneously and multiple times per day. How many social media tabs do you have open now? Are you a social media multitasker? Do you become agitated when you cannot check a social media account? You are not alone. Some of us manage most, if not all, of our social relationships and personal relationships online.

Although social media is a fact of life and certainly helps to enhance our connectivity, we don't want to lose ourselves.

We often feel scattered in our day-to-day lives. Attaining a steady mental focus is becoming more and more difficult. Lack of sleep, stress, poor diet and nutrition, and constant distractions (such as social media) affect our ability to focus and concentrate. This has an impact on our work, relationships, and most other aspects of our lives.

Learning to concentrate deeply is important to our mental health and well-being. Practicing dharana teaches us to focus our attention fully on one subject and expands our potential to engage directly with the world rather than withdraw from it.

Tap into Your Personal Presence

Personal presence is a differentiating factor in career success. It is not an innate skill—anyone can learn it. Try the four exercises below.

Manage your mind-body balance through balanced breathing. Use a balanced inhale/exhale breathing cycle: simply inhale for five seconds, and then exhale for five seconds. If you do this regularly throughout the day, it will help bring your nervous system into balance and allow you to better focus your attention.

Monitor your body language. Are you open in your body language and receptivity? Do you make good eye contact? Is your body language aligned with your verbal presence? Check your posture both sitting and standing. Are you slumped over, or are you tall and straight? Imagine a string attached to the crown of your head, gently lifting your head and spine upward toward the ceiling. Good posture conveys confidence. This may be challenging at first. But the more you make an effort to check in on your body language, the more naturally it will come to you—you'll find yourself taking a moment to straighten up at different points throughout the day. You can also consider asking a trusted colleague to take a photo of you while you're working without you realizing it so you know how you're sitting at your desk. Just be prepared for a rude awakening—we can be dramatically slumped when we aren't mindful of it!

- **At the end of each day ask yourself: How did I show up?** Is your mind filled with chitter-chatter when speaking to others? How effectively did you communicate today? Are you really connecting with them or talking at them? Were you fully engaged? Notice how others react to you. Work to show up in the way that you want others to perceive you.

- **Live in the moment and be present.** Focus your attention on one thing at a time rather than constantly trying to multitask. It's harder than it seems in our 24/7 world, but it's well worth the effort. When we give our full attention to what we are doing in the present, we let go of outcomes and enjoy the moment, prolonging its value.

Self-Reflection

1. Can you pay attention and focus on your key goals for a day? If not, what gets in the way?

2. How often do you disconnect from your phone? Your computer? Your email?

3. Can you focus only on what you are doing now?

4. Do you feel more successful and in control when you focus only on what you are doing *now*?

5. What are three ways that will help you focus and perform better at work?

6. How do you show up? Do you appear poised and confident? How would you describe your personal presence?

7

Meditating Toward
a Balanced Mind

*"In the attitude of silence the soul finds the path
in a clearer light, and what is elusive and deceptive
resolves itself into crystal clearness. Our life is a long
and arduous quest after Truth."*
—Mahatma Gandhi

I admit that before I first engaged in meditation I thought it was a weird practice. When I thought of people meditating I pictured them sitting still and breathing with their eyes closed, then they would open their eyes, get up, and go about their business. What was the big deal? I wasn't sure of the point and doubted whether I would get anything out of it personally. A few of my skeptical friends actually called it "hippie bullshit." Others called it the "New Age fad" (a funny idea, as people have been practicing meditation in different ways for thousands of years!). However, I began to read and learn about people who had made remarkable shifts in their lives through meditation practice. I remained hesitant that it could help me to better manage my career and my personal life, but I figured: Why not try it? What did I have to lose?

Meditation and mindfulness (the practice of paying attention to the present moment in a focused and nonjudgmental way) have inundated the popular media over the past few years and become increasingly mainstream. They are now watchwords in contemporary business trends, and celebrities like mega-athlete LeBron James, singer-songwriter Madonna, and actor-producer Jerry Seinfeld are all public proponents.

I recently saw large table with a sign for "Mindfulness" at a local Barnes and Noble—everything from books to cards to games to CDs to help with the process. I have wondered whether the increased uptake of these ancient practices is a reaction to our "always on" lifestyle or perhaps a response to social media marketing and our desire to "look and act the part." Nevertheless, the popularity of this practice is still a rich opportunity for those who genuinely want to develop personal insights, greater awareness, and experience positive change. Such change, if actually adopted by our popular culture, could ultimately lead to a more benevolent society. And you don't need to spend money on anything from the Mindfulness table to start practicing meditation and mindfulness in your life at work or at home.

Meditation is a word that has come to be used loosely and inaccurately, with many associated misperceptions. It is often viewed as a practice to escape reality, which includes daydreaming or fantasizing. Others believe they need to "quiet their minds" before they can learn to meditate. Still others believe meditation is about creating a blank mind so they can think about nothing. In reality meditation is not about emptying your mind, getting rid of your thoughts, or contemplating your big toe. Yogic meditation—*dhyana*—is a deep and rich practice with a millennia-old history behind it, but you don't need to know everything about it to make this age-old practice part of your life today.

Briefly, *dhyana* is a Sanskrit term that means attention or contemplation. Meditation is a practice for resting the mind and attaining a state of consciousness totally different from the normal waking state. In meditation the mind is clear, relaxed with a one-pointed, inward focus. Ultimately the mind becomes silent and is not distracted by the external world. In the words of famous yogi B. K. S. Iyengar, when a yogi meditates, "The flow of concentration is uninterrupted" like "the filament in an electric bulb," revealing "the light that shines in his own heart."

Maybe you don't care about flow or revealing the light that shines in your heart. That's perfectly fine. I'm certainly not sitting in an ashram practicing yoga for hours on end! You don't need to be a hippie type, a vegan, or even own yoga pants to reap the rewards of a regular practice of breathing and finding greater calm, focus, and awareness in your busy day. There is an increasing body of research on the health benefits associated with the practice of meditation that should interest you a *little*, including stress reduction, decreased anxiety, decreased depression, pain reduction (both physical and psychological), and improved quality of sleep. Additional physiological benefits include reduced blood pressure and heart rate as well as decreased cortisol, cholesterol, lactate, and epinephrine. (This decrease in epinephrine helps to modulate the "fight or flight" response by decreasing sympathetic overstimulation.)

Still not convinced? Research has also shown that, when practiced daily, meditation has a wide range of mental benefits. Meditation improves cerebral blood flow, leading to increased efficiency in the brain's executive attention network, which translates into improved response time and better efficiency in attention-related task completion. Neuroscientists have found that meditators actually shift their brain activity to different areas of the cerebral cortex; brain waves in the stress-prone right frontal cortex move to the calmer left frontal cortex. In other words, you'll think faster, better, and be more productive.

If you're *still* not interested, consider that although there are many forms of mediation, you can benefit from a simple practice that takes five to ten minutes per day. That's it! Now, you may be thinking, *How am I going to find even five minutes in my day when it seems like there is no time to begin with?* Yet if you give it a try, you might find that meditation seems to *add* time to your day. This is what happened to me—I didn't think I had time, but somehow I forced myself to devote a few minutes per day to meditation and found after about a month that I had more control over my mind and spent less time on distracting activities. You heard me right—*a few minutes per day.*

There are many different methods of meditation and ways to practice, but the most important aspect of meditation is that you temporarily withdraw your attention from the outside world and thoughts related to it in order to focus on a chosen theme, such as your breath or a mantra. The common key to almost all meditation practices is silence

Try This in Two Minutes
What One Breath Feels Like

If a formal meditation practice seems like a daunting task, simply pay attention to what one breath feels like. Anyone can do this at any time.

Take a long, smooth, and slow breath.

Feel the sensations of that one breath flowing in and out with your inhale and exhale. Notice the sensations in your nostrils, your face, your rib cage, and the rise and fall of your abdomen.

and harmonization of your thoughts and judgments. Concentrating on a single point of focus and letting your thoughts flow of their own accord will help lead you to an inner stillness that supports you as you deal with the stresses of everyday life.

I try to devote at least five minutes in the morning and evening to meditate, but I don't always achieve that. *Whenever* I can find a few moments to pause, minimize distractions, and focus on my breathing, I do. I don't worry about where I'm doing it or whether I'm doing it "correctly." My version of meditation is really about practicing my ability to pause so I don't react when life gets crazy. We all face hectic issues at home and in the workplace. Strengthening our comfort level with quiet moments can greatly help us to handle whatever problems arise and to better trust our ability to manage matters without creating extra stress with our own reactions.

Just a few minutes of daily meditation has taught me so much about myself and how I handle any situation—from last-minute requests to travel abroad, to speaking in front of a large audience, or to the time I came home and found water gushing everywhere from a major leak in a water supply pipe! Instead of feeling overwhelmed and out of control, I sit and breathe, then find a solution.

Meditation has created space: with a quieter mind I have space to think, to center myself, and to better focus and self-regulate. I find myself less anxious, less irritable, and more resilient in the face of stress. I can put unending demands and stressors in a "container" and compartmentalize them, which has allowed me to deal with them more slowly and focus on my most important decisions rather than everything at once. Stressful events have less chance of snowballing into situations I find unmanageable. If sitting on the floor with my eyes closed is how I do this, so be it! I think we could all use a little time to unplug and refocus.

Connection Is the Key

Why is yoga so healing? Many of us were conditioned during our youth to believe that parts of us are unacceptable. This may lead us to feel pain and become disconnected from our self and from our own body. In yoga we're uncovering what exists inside of us, and we learn to see that we are whole and complete as we are. The identification of yoga with wholeness and completeness dates back to Vedic philosophy and the foundations of yoga. The ancient Sanskrit mantra *sohum*, or "I am that" (*so* means "I am," and *hum* means "that") is the affirmation that the individual self can identify as one with the universe. Many Vedic scholars have interpreted the "that" in the mantra to represent the universe. Through awareness of our oneness we begin to let go of what no longer serves us.

The idea of being one with the universe allows us to feel safe, supported, and protected. We are better able to embrace our inherent nature—perfect, whole, complete. I personally meditate using the mantra *sohum*. I find it to be a good way to anchor myself—to quiet and focus my mind and to relax my body.

Leaders at America's most prominent companies, such as Apple, Google, and even General Mills and Ford Motor Company, practice meditation and actively encourage meditation for their employees as an inexpensive, scientifically proven way to build resilience and enhance overall well-being. Across the Silicon Valley and beyond, silence and contemplation have become the new caffeine, a fuel that ostensibly unlocks productivity and creative bursts.

Each year thousands of employees at Google take company courses on mindfulness meditation, the increasingly prevalent practice of having a "balanced awareness" of what's happening around you. The most popular class since its inception in 2007 is called "Search Inside Yourself." The course teaches employees to breathe mindfully, listen more to their coworkers, and enhance their emotional intelligence. Chade Meng-Tan, a Singapore-born engineer and former Google employee founded the course. Meng-Tan has said, "I'm not interested in bringing Buddhism to Google. I am interested in helping people at Google find the key to happiness."

Many prominent leaders well outside of Silicon Valley also credit meditation for their equanimity and poise. Management and consulting firm McKinsey & Co. might seem like a strange place to find people meditating, but the company is embracing meditation as a way to keep employees healthy and happy. Manish Chopra, a principal in McKinsey's New York office, states, "Most of today's workers—and senior executives perhaps most of all—lack what they need, whether it's meditation or a different approach, to balance and offset the demands of their 'anywhere, everywhere' roles in today's corporations."

Okay, so it's clear that meditation offers a whole host of benefits, but *what's the point* in practical terms? The point of meditation is to gain control over your most precious tool: your mind and your attention.

The state of your mind is the most determining factor in your success and happiness. The state of your mind affects your overall health.

Meditation means training the mind to become still and to regain power and control over your thoughts. We all have what is called the "monkey mind," or mind chatter that flits from one subject to the next, intruding our thoughts when we need or want to concentrate and keeping us from focusing on any given task at hand.

Typical mind chatter feels like this in your head:

- reading off a laundry list of to-do items

- listing real and imaginary fears

- recalling hurtful things that have happened in the past

- judging the present

- brooding about the past

- creating catastrophic "what if" scenarios of the future

10 Percent Happier

Those who practice mediation are generally happier and calmer than those who don't—about 10 percent happier, according to ABC news correspondent Dan Harris. After having a nationally televised panic attack on *Good Morning America*, Harris knew he needed help. Despite much hesitation and resistance, he tried meditation and found its benefits to be unparalleled. In his book *10% Happier: How I Tamed the Voice in My Head, Reduced Stress Without Losing My Edge, and Found Self-Help that Actually Works—A True Story*, Harris suggests that although meditation won't solve all your problems, it will make you about 10 percent happier. Now, it's not a grand promise, but it is an honest one. And who wouldn't want to feel even just a little bit happier and more relaxed each day?

Mind chatter makes it nearly impossible to slow down and enjoy the present, much less focus on an important task at hand. Meditation helps us respond rather than react. It provides a fraction-of-a-second delay, just enough time to reconsider whether you really want to do or say what the voice in your head is urging. In meditation we focus our attention on our breath or a mantra. Thoughts will intrude, but we let them pass rather than indulge them. In so doing we learn to tame the "monkey mind." By mastering the ability to put your attention on the things you want (and keep it there) and to remove it from things that are negative or not serving you, you gain the ability to create what you want both in yourself and in your life.

So how do you actually meditate? Here are six easy steps:

1 **Pause.** Turn off your cell phone, shut down your computer, and give yourself a few moments of quiet. Even if you only achieve this step, you'll feel an immediate physical impact: your brain activity is less frenzied.

2 **Find a comfortable seated position.** You don't need to sit cross-legged on the floor (unless you want to), but find a comfortable yet firm chair or cushion and sit upright with a straight spine and your chin level to the floor. Don't stiffen—your spine has a normal curvature, so let it be there. Relax your shoulders away from your ears. Situate your upper arms parallel to your upper body, with the palms of your hands on your legs. Specific hand placement is not necessary. If you don't have a quiet, private space in your workplace, perhaps there is a space nearby—a library or a café, even your car—or perhaps you can find time to practice in your home. The simpler, the better, as your physical environment should not be a distraction.

3 **Focus on your breathing.** As you sit and begin to relax, gently close or hood your eyes and observe the in-and-out flow of your breath, staying

focused on that sensation. Breathe from your diaphragm, not your chest—you'll know the difference when your belly starts to move up and down with your breath. Think of how a child or even a dog breathes naturally and fully from their abdomen. (See page 110 in Chapter 4 for a refresher on diaphragmatic breathing.) When you notice your mind wandering, return your attention to your breath. Take a few deep, full breaths, and exhale loudly, expelling any extraneous noise from your head. Eventually you will begin to feel your whole body release and move in rhythm with your breathing. But "eventually" may take a while. Try to observe your thoughts without reacting to them. Return to your breath, over and over again, without judgment or expectation. Remember: it's a practice.

4 **Gently lift your gaze or open your eyes.** Take a moment to notice how your body feels and observe your thoughts and emotions. Has there been a shift? Perhaps write a few notes in your journal.

5 **Aim to practice every day.** Meditation is like training any other muscle—you need to keep at it for it to work. Remember: a meditation session can be a short as a few minutes. For those of you who don't have a minute to spare, schedule it into your calendar and find time whenever you can. There is no magic formula here, but you'll soon start to notice the benefits of your practice, which will keep you motivated to continue.

6 **Minimize your expectations.** If you are attached to goals and time frames, meditation will be difficult for you. Meditation is a process. Try not to become "the world's best meditator." In the beginning focus on creating the habit of meditation. Resist the urge to continually evaluate yourself. Let go of self-criticism, comparison, and expectations as soon as they arise. The process will feel more wholesome and enjoyable.

As I mentioned before, I try to find time to sit and meditate for a few minutes in the mornings and evenings, but I also pause whenever I can—if a meeting is starting late, I might sit and breathe while everyone gathers. If I'm stuck in traffic, I can breathe in the car (I keep my eyes open). Integrating these pause moments into your regular routine will help you strengthen your ability to find calm and handle stressful moments with better clarity and confidence. And if you miss a day or two, don't worry—just remember to stop and breathe whenever and wherever you can.

Organizations don't change. People do. What gets someone to make that behavioral shift? There are limits of an external model, whether it's positive or negative—bonuses, micromanaging, and an overall corporate culture can only do so much. Most of us need to enhance our own self-awareness—we will only make lasting changes if we actually have the desire to change for our own individual reasons. Meditation can unlock a higher level of self- and social awareness. Both of these are powerful tools for building teams, being creative, and making clear decisions.

Through my meditation practice I have experienced a shift in how I focus my energies. I have better control of my thoughts and actions. I observe more and react less. I avoid knee-jerk reactions to incoming stimuli and situations that I perceive as negative. Even in situations in which I do not succeed, I am able better to reflect on "why" without reacting. Did my ego get in the way? Was I too results driven in the short term? Did the issue bring up my own insecurities?

Using the mind to watch the mind (thinking about one's thinking) and ultimately to change how the mind works is known as metacognition. More precisely, metacognition refers to the processes used to

Ten Simple Meditation Tips
for Beginners

When you first begin to practice meditation you may not feel anything really change. And if you can't quiet your thoughts, you aren't alone. Here are ten useful tips to start incorporating meditation into your day.

1. **You can meditate anywhere, anytime.** The key is focusing on your breath as you inhale and exhale.

2. **If you want to do a more formal meditation practice** and it is difficult for you to sit, lie down.

3. **You don't need to close your eyes.** Just soften your gaze, and let your eyes fall where they may. This may help you to better tolerate the practice and avoid falling asleep.

4. **Start with breathing meditations**—they are the simplest and don't require any special props.

5. **Begin meditation for five minutes.** If five minutes seems like an interminable amount of time, give yourself permission to start with less time—even one minute. Or try the exercise What One Breath Feels Like on page 158.

6. **Set a timer.** By setting a timer you will be less inclined to look at a clock and less worried about things you are missing, as this is your scheduled time. You can relax and focus on your meditation practice without worrying that you will go over time and miss something important.

7. **Let other people know that you are serious about your meditation practice.** They will be less likely to interrupt you, and they may want to join you!

8. **Find a meditation community**. This is not required but is a great way to spend time with like-minded people who will help to support your personal practice. Consider doing a twenty-one-day or thirty-day meditation challenge with a friend to get into the habit of meditation.

9. **Don't try to be perfect.** There is no right or wrong way to meditate.

10. **Don't give up.** Things will undoubtedly come up from time to time that will challenge your willingness and desire to stay with the practice. Keep going. As you become more consistent with a daily practice (remember: it can be just a few minutes), the less effort it will take to keep it up.

plan, monitor, and assess one's understanding and performance. All leaders face challenges involving high levels of novelty and ambiguity that require creative problem solving, social judgment, and knowledge of the task, organization, and people. Metacognitive abilities of monitoring and adapting cognition can improve a leader's self-awareness as well as his ability to understand and influence others.

Still not quite sure about meditation? Fair enough. But let me ask you this: What exactly do you have to lose by giving it a try? Not enough time to meditate? How about this: take note of all the unproductive time that you spend in front of a screen in one week (TV, smartphone, computer, or tablet). The following week use a small portion of that time to meditate. Just that small first step will take you a long way toward less stress and more peace in your life.

Self-Reflection

1. What habitual thoughts occupy your mind?

2. Describe what are the obstacles to your meditation practice?

3. Despite obstacles, are you willing to do and to stick with the practice?

4. If not now, when? Why wait?

5. What changes do you see in yourself since you have been practicing meditation? What changes do others see?

6. With your daily meditation practice (even if two minutes per day): Do you feel happier? Less stressed? Better able to concentrate? More self-aware?

8

Taking the Leader's Path

"What man actually needs is not a tensionless state but rather the striving and struggling for some goal worthy of him."
—Victor Frankl

How does one truly become a great leader and, in turn, inspire others? In business just because someone is hired or promoted as a leader (or appoints herself as head of a new startup) doesn't suddenly teach that person how to lead effectively, which any disenchanted subordinate knows all too well. Although some people can naturally take charge and others seem to have an easy chemistry at the helm of a large group, becoming a successful leader is a profound and demanding transformation.

My field is medicine, and we all spend years learning and practicing our skills to get our MDs. But even after eight-plus years of college and medical school our education is far from complete. A freshly minted doctor typically spends time in residency and possibly a fellowship pursuing advanced training in his or her specialty of choice. After all that rigorous training he or she may join a practice or perhaps be installed as the leader of a multidisciplinary team, in both cases charged with delivering the highest quality care to patients. And even then it takes time to fully master the responsibilities, skills, and professionalism required of a physician. The point is that these skills are taught, learned, practiced, and assimilated—no one is born a doctor, just as no one is born a great leader.

I believe that *anyone* can learn to be a leader, regardless of their beginnings or professional choice. A solid yogic practice is the perfect training ground for this metamorphosis, and the skills and practices you read about in the previous chapters are the ultimate tools for successful leaders in the modern workplace.

The eight limbs of yoga discussed in the Yoga Sutras of Patañjali are actually a path, beginning with a moral foundation, traveling through the body and into the mind and then culminating with *samadhi*. The highest stage in meditation, samadhi is an experience of ultimate presence and true alertness. The yogi who achieves samadhi is quite literally transformed so that he experiences oneness with the universe. He is in a state of being totally aware of the present moment, one pointedness of mind.

Achieving samadhi may sound a bit esoteric, but it's really more commonplace than you might think. You have probably already experienced it without even realizing it—it's the feeling of being totally absorbed in your work—or play—where you experience total connectedness with the subject at hand. Things become effortless, and time either seems to stand still or hours suddenly pass by very quickly. Some people describe it as being "on a roll," while others might say they "forgot themselves" in the process.

In sports it's often called "being in the zone." After a great performance athletes have often described a state of feeling invincible, as if the game slowed down, the crowd fell silent, and they achieved an incredible focus in order to score the point or finish first.

As I've mentioned, the notable Hungarian psychologist Mihaly Csikszentmihalyi has called this state "flow." This is where our best performance, our best ideas, and our highest levels of satisfaction come from. We act effortlessly. We are strong, alert, and at the peak of our abilities. We have a loss of self-consciousness. In the flow state we're not thinking about doing it; we're just doing it. However, when we look back on what we were doing, we recall it as enjoyable or even exhilarating—even if it's work. Although this state of flow requires significant effort leading up to that moment, we must also be able to let go of control in order to trust our natural abilities. Flow involves a dynamic interplay between focus and softening, effort and effortlessness.

A growing body of scientific evidence indicates that this type of flow is highly correlated with happiness. People who experience a regular state of flow also develop other positive traits, including enhanced concentration, self-esteem, and performance. Think of a colleague or friend who not only seems to genuinely enjoy their job but has also thrived in their industry. What characteristics do they exude?

Creating the space to achieve great things is only possible if we take away so much of the busyness that's a pervasive part of our daily lives. I've spent countless hours on the Metro-North train (the local commuter train to New York City), Amtrak, and airplanes keenly aware that I'm the only one not tapping away on my phone or computer! Granted, I may still be thinking about work or upcoming events, but I try my best not to allow extraneous distractions to clutter my head. When I put my electronic devices away, it is often in these quiet moments when an idea sparks and I am inspired to follow through with it.

Synchronicity

We have all had perfect moments when events could never be predicted, let alone controlled but remarkably seem to guide us along our path. Swiss psychiatrist and psychologist Carl Jung termed this phenomenon *synchronicity*, defining it as an "acausal connecting (togetherness) principle," a "meaningful coincidence of two or more events, where something other than the probability of chance is involved." In his book *Synchronicity: The Inner Path of Leadership* Joseph Jaworski explores the capacity we have to sense and, in a way, predict the emerging future and to shape it rather than simply respond to forces at large.

I have been involved with the health, wellness, fitness, and/or yoga communities for all of my adult life. I have come to understand my ultimate mission in medicine is to promote disease prevention and healthier lifestyles worldwide. I look for creative outlets such as writing and public speaking to support these intentions and to deliver my messages. Good psychological and physical health supports effective leadership. So I decided to marry my interests in health, wellness, yoga, and leadership to write this book. Other people emerged to support my efforts in this new world of publishing—a publishing guru, a literary agent, and a major publisher believed in me. And now this book is in your hands.

A book deal may not be your goal, but you can start to create an environment in which to pursue more meaningful connections in your own life. Whatever your hobby may be, look for a local group or class. By actively engaging your passion, you're nurturing that creative or inspired side of yourself in a group setting, where you may meet interesting people or be present for new opportunities.

How much more could be possible if we operated from this state on a regular basis instead of always being connected? In this chapter we will discuss a few simple ways to cultivate greater opportunities for samadhi in your home or workplace.

Set the Stage

We all have constant mind chatter in our daily lives. Our "monkey minds" typically jump in and out throughout the day with a running commentary—we find ourselves judging, critiquing, and assigning meaning to things that don't need our constant attention. In order to encourage samadhi arising within us, we need to temporarily quiet this chatter so our senses can be engaged in the task at hand.

At work we must eliminate as many physical distractions as possible. The simple act of shutting your door, turning off email alerts, and sending phone calls to voicemail sets the stage for fewer distractions.

One almost-immediate way is to interrupt your monkey mind midsentence and distract it by reciting a mantra. When you recite a mantra you draw in your scattered attention and focus it on a word, phrase, or sound. I typically use the words "quiet" or "calm" as mantras, repeating them silently to myself. In less than a minute I find myself more focused and relaxed. You may find other words that can serve as mantras and reminders to yourself.

Breathe Mindfully and Slowly

Samadhi cannot be entered intentionally—it arises on its own. When you slow your breath, your mind automatically follows. Breathing slowly and intentionally brings the body and mind in focus together. Whenever possible take a few minutes to practice your style of meditation, whether it's at home before your commute, once you get to the office, or during an afternoon break. These "pause" moments and a focus on your breathing will help you truly clear your head of distractions and allow you to create space for new thoughts and ideas. Revisit the breathing exercises on pages 109–115 for a few quick ones you can do in nearly any situation.

Let Go of Control

Don't force progress or focus only on answers and outcomes; instead, turn your thoughts inward and focus on deepening your awareness of the situation—start asking yourself questions like: What's really going on beneath all the noise? You may find it's easier to resolve things from a place of inner connectedness.

Work-related flow includes three primary elements: total immersion in an activity; enjoyment or positive judgments about that activity; and intrinsic motivation. (Performing the activity for the pleasure and satisfaction of doing it, not simply for the salary or some other benefit). A strong sense of work-related flow is associated with increased job satisfaction, enthusiasm, and contentment. This makes sense because if you enjoy your job, you'll go in every day with a positive attitude and a feeling of self-worth when you return home. It's especially true for achievement-oriented people who desire a balance of high skill and high challenge and are rewarded with greater positive mood, interest in their tasks, and better performance.

Given the many opportunities to feel this incredible state of flow, why do we so often choose passive or mind-numbing activities like watching TV or playing computer games in our scarce free time? Well, sometimes we're just looking to zone out rather than to be in the

In May 2016, Facebook reported that its users spend an average of fifty minutes a day on its combined Facebook, Instagram, and Messenger platforms (not counting the messaging app WhatsApp). I realize certain industries require employees to maintain an active social media presence, and certainly there is value in following news or trends online, but consider whether you're really allowing yourself to flow and create space for new ideas or simply giving in to procrastination? What if you spent thirty minutes or more every day taking a walk outside and brainstorming? Or, better yet, devoting even *half* the time you engage in social media to your yoga practice instead?

zone. Even if the activity is designed as downtime, it can be valuable. Csikszentmihalyi says that we must find the activity important—even if only in a small way—for it to produce flow. Think about things that bring you great satisfaction. Happiness, engagement, and meaning are needed to sustain long-term interest. If we don't enjoy an activity, we'll eventually burn out; if we don't find the activity meaningful, it will ultimately feel empty.

With so much external noise and so many responsibilities, it's more important than ever to reserve at least a few minutes each day to tune in to ourselves, honor the energy inside of us, and tap into it using our breath and focus. That is the not-so-secret source of great leadership and inspiration.

Sometimes it's hard to find those moments to devote to your practice, but with some creative thinking you can make use of little gifts of downtime. For example, if you're traveling, you can do yoga in the airplane while thirty thousand feet above the ground, and there are significant benefits of a short practice! You may want to consider trying a few flight-friendly yoga poses to reverse some of the damaging effects of extended periods of sitting on a plane (or in a train or subway car). These poses don't require much space, so you should avoid curious on-lookers if you are self-conscious. I travel a lot, and I find the poses below to have significant benefits. They:

- release muscle tension,

- relax the mind,

- soothe the nervous system,

- decrease anxiety,

- reduce risk of deep vein thrombosis, and

- help you feel refreshed when engaging in postflight activities.

Eight Effective In-Flight Yoga Poses You Can Do in Your Seat

Neck Stretches

With your head straight and gaze forward, inhale while you look ahead. Exhale, and look to your right. Inhale, and look ahead. Exhale, and look to your left. Repeat.

Shoulder Lift

With your head straight and gaze forward, inhale, and raise shoulders toward your ears. Exhale, lower shoulders, and completely let go. Repeat.

Neck Rolls

Start with your head straight and gaze forward. Gently tip your head to your left. Then roll your head back into an extended position with your eyes facing the ceiling. With your head back, roll your head to your right. Next, roll your head so your chin faces down and a little toward the front of your neck. This stretches the muscles at the back of your neck and contracts those in front. Finish the movement by bringing your head back up to the start position. Repeat.

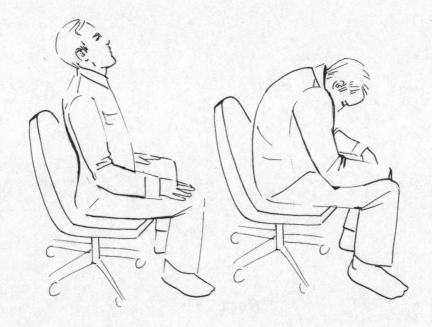

Seated Cat-Cow Pose

Sit on the edge of your seat, with a comfortable distance between your knees and with your ankles in line with your knees. Place your hands on your thighs, and as you inhale, draw your chest forward and your shoulders back. As you exhale, round your spine and draw your shoulders forward. Look down toward your navel, relaxing your neck and head. Repeat five to six times.

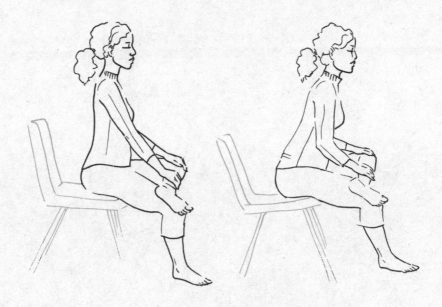

Back Release Pose

You might consider removing your shoes for this pose. While seated upright on your seat, cross your left ankle over your right knee, leaving your right foot on the floor. Keep your left foot flexed (pull your toes up toward your body) to help protect the knee. Breathe deeply, and take your attention to your lower back. Fold over, and bring your torso forward to deepen the stretch. Hold in this pose, taking eight to ten deep breaths. Repeat with the right foot.

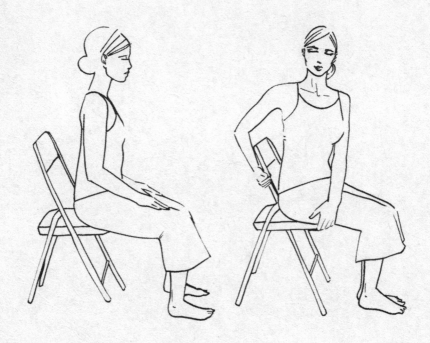

Seated Spinal Twist

Sit up tall, and grab the sides of your seat. Inhale, and grow taller. Exhale, and twist your torso to your right, gazing to the right as well, and hold for ten to twenty seconds. Return to center, and repeat on the other side.

Thigh Lifts

To strengthen and improve circulation in your legs while seated, lift one leg at a time, imagining that you are lifting the middle of your thigh up to the ceiling. Keep your back straight while you are doing this, and pull your belly button inward to engage your abdominal muscles.

Seated Savasana (Corpse Pose)

Savasana comes from two words: *Sava*, or corpse, and *asana*, or pose.

It implies a depth of release that goes beyond simple relaxation. Sitting comfortably in a chair, let go of all muscle tension. Let go of the noise and other distractions. When your thoughts come, let them go. Rest deeply.

Practicing Samadhi

We enter the workplace—as interns, assistants, trainees—and are often thrown into the deep end without a life vest. Even if we've been trained to swim, it's a daunting experience. In the first phase of our careers, as in the first phase of our training as yogis, most of our energy is spent developing fundamental skills. We learn to perform tasks in a timely manner, to be conscientious, to exceed expectations. Eventually we are trusted with greater and greater responsibilities. And it's important not to forget to experience samadhi whenever possible. Sound esoteric? Not really. Samadhi occurs when we experience a complete absorption and connectedness with whatever we are doing at the time. When we achieve samadhi at work we maintain a deeper connection with our job and the people around us. It doesn't matter what kind of work you do or what your current position is—you can experience a greater feeling of enjoyment, elation, and perhaps even bliss by cultivating these personal practices:

⇒ Take responsibility when you succeed—and especially when you fail.

⇒ Go the extra mile, even if you're not expected or required to do so.

⇒ Care about doing a great job, no matter how trivial the task.

⇒ Embrace challenges as opportunities to develop new skills.

⇒ Handle difficult situations with grace.

⇒ Appreciate opportunities and those who are willing to support and mentor you.

⋛ Make the best of things; it's better than the alternative.

⋛ Be consistent. Constant steady effort is a key to success.

⋛ Maintain a positive attitude, especially when circumstances are difficult.

⋛ Offer kind words and inspiration to others in need.

⋛ Seek out others who exude a zeal for life; their spirit will rub off on you.

Up until this point our yogic practice has centered on personal development, but eventually we must turn outward. As Marshall Goldsmith writes, successful people become great leaders when they learn to shift the focus from themselves outward to others. Goldsmith says we can all find (and retain) our mojo—a funny slang word that really means the moment when we do something that's purposeful, powerful, and positive and the rest of the world recognizes it. Our professional and personal mojo is impacted by four key factors: identity (who you think you are), achievement (what you have done lately), reputation (who other people think you are) and acceptance (what you can change and when you need to just "let it go").

You don't need to be a great athlete, celebrity, or powerful CEO to find your mojo. After my morning yoga and fitness routine I stop by my local Starbucks around 7 a.m. to pick up my coffee. Some of the baristas simply ask for my order and generally serve me politely but without much eye contact. But there's a certain crew who greets me with enthusiasm: "Good morning! How are you doing? Great to see you today! Beautiful day! Do you want your usual today?" This positive

From Controlling
to Connecting

I have struggled with perfectionistic qualities for many years.
As a team leader I wanted everything done quickly and done
right. I set the pace for the team by imparting my views and
my ways and involving myself in key decisions across functional lines. I thought I was making things *easier* for my team
by giving them good direction and guidance. The team was
hitting milestones well, but I began to feel personally isolated
and that team members were working in *spite* of me, not in
support of me. I had no idea why—I really cared about my
work and serving patients. I also cared about the team members. Why did I feel so alienated? With the help of a good
coach I began to see that I was too controlling. My team
members did not feel empowered and were reluctant to share
their thoughts and ideas with me or to bring them forward in
meetings. This was not my intent—I wanted everyone on the
team to be recognized and to have a voice, but I was not acting in a way that supported this view. I began to get to know
my team members better and to make sure I asked for their
ideas, listened to and implemented those ideas, and gave
proper credit. I worked—and still do—to evolve myself from a
controlling to a connecting leader. Great leaders care about
people and results—in that order.

spirit—their mojo—radiates directly outward to me and the other customers, and it helps start my day on an upbeat, energetic note. I frequent this particular café in part because I always look forward to these
brief but meaningful interactions.

Many people in service industries use mojo to their advantage at
work. In my current position I travel frequently in airplanes, giving me
the chance to interact with hundreds of flight attendants. Most are
dedicated, professional, and service oriented. A few are grumpy and act
like they would rather be anywhere else than on the plane. A handful
are just fantastic at what they do—keeping the passengers safe, organized, and smiling for the duration of the flight—*especially* if there are
long delays. Now *that's* mojo. All these flight attendants are doing basically the same activity, at the same time, for the same company, yet
the message that each is sending to the world about their experience is
completely different.

Business models built on a hierarchal structure with organized leadership and a guiding principle based on the "bottom line" are no
longer popular. These models do not prioritize people—you can down-
size them, rank order them, get rid of the bottom 10 percent, and take
other liberties because in this system people are perceived as commodi-
ties. Leaders are now beginning to understand that building a company
on connected, organic leadership and ideology of wholeness, not simply
the "bottom line," is actually a recipe for success. This model's guiding
principles are based on people and relationships. The skills and values
we learn from our practice of yoga go hand in hand with the success of
these principles.

Prioritizing people compels leaders to look internally, create a
deeper connection with their employees, and develop a higher

> ## *Try This in Two Minutes*
>
> Observe two different colleagues or employees doing exactly the same job at the same time, even if it's just the way they attend a meeting. Note their different styles and approaches and the reaction they get or the way they accomplish the task at hand. Does one have more mojo than the other? Do they both have mojo but express it in different ways? What can you learn from observing others' mojos, and how can you incorporate the aspects that feel right for you?

awareness as a company. They realize that profit comes from creating a sustainably motivating environment for people who, in turn, will take care of customers and grow the business. Leadership expert Ken Blanchard is a pioneer of people-centered leadership and defines it as a holistic approach to unleashing the power and potential of people in organizations. He states, "A leader's objective is to develop people's confidence and competence, so that they gain self-reliance—which leads to results." The proof is in, well, the profits: just look at companies such as Google, Facebook, Nordstrom's, Disney, and Southwest Airlines—they all utilize this philosophy.

In 1980 the US Olympic men's hockey team was set to play against the Soviet men's team in the Winter Olympics in Lake Placid, New York. At the time the Soviet team was the undisputed powerhouse in men's hockey. No one expected the US team to have any chance of beating the Soviet team: the Americans were a mix of amateur and collegiate players, and the Russians had won the gold medal in six of the seven previous Olympic Games. Before the game the US coach, Herb Brooks, read his players a statement he had written out on a piece of paper, telling them, "You were born to be a player. You were meant to be here. This moment is yours."

As the games unfolded, the US team beat the Soviet team in the medal-round game, and the victory became one of the most iconic moments not only of the Olympics but also in American sports history— it's often referred to as the "Miracle on Ice." Ultimately the US team took home the gold medal by beating Finland in their final match of the tournament.

This is one of my favorite sports-leadership examples because it shows so clearly how fostering a sense of confidence and belief in a team can inspire them to achieve great things. The same can hold true whether you are managing a small group, leading a large company, or even hoping to inspire yourself as an independent contractor. By fostering flow, finding your mojo, and putting people first, you will create a dynamic environment in which to succeed.

One of the most powerful enlightened leaders today is a sixty-three-year-old South Indian woman, Mata Amritanandamayi, known as Amma, or "Mother," for her selfless love and compassion toward all human beings. Amma has dedicated her life to alleviating the pain and suffering of the poor and to building a concerned and caring society. She facilitates public events and retreats throughout the world and concludes her appearances by embracing attendees. Amma has been known to sit on stage for more than fifteen hours, and she has hugged more than 34 million devotees over the past thirty years. Amma's global network of charity organizations, Embracing the World, exists in forty countries and provides food, housing, education, and medical services for the poor. Pulitzer prize–winning author Alice Walker has said, "Amma presents the kind of leadership we need for our planet to survive. This is the most heroic person I've probably ever met." Amma's purity of heart and her unique blend of courage, humility, and caring has had great impact. She radiates love.

I always wanted to become a physician. I can truly say that I love my career in medicine and that I have never regretted my choice. It has been a privilege to serve patients with life-limiting or life-threatening illnesses. Whether during one-on-one interactions with patients, in forums with patient advocacy groups, or during high-stakes situations in my current role in drug development, I have found that the bigger the challenge, the more focused and calm I have become. I have learned to move into a low gear to tune out everything around me, to think clearly and in a logical and organized fashion, often making my best and most creative decisions in high-stakes situations. In these moments I am in a state of flow, or samadhi.

But it wasn't always that way. I graduated from medical school at the young age of twenty-five. For a moment I felt on top of the world, but then reality set in. My inability to navigate a complex bureaucracy and an intricate matrix of relationships became apparent and remained so through my residency, fellowship, and well into my post-training years. My entire education had focused on teaching me how to work with patients, and I felt completely unprepared and inept as a leader. My years of medical training were almost exclusively focused on my clinical skill set. That knowledge base alone was overwhelming—and certainly insufficient once I had transitioned to my first postfellowship role as an attending physician in an academic medical center.

I recognized that the act of seeing patients and delivering a treatment plan is dependent on a whole team of people. I was expected to be an effective team leader right out of the gate but was never taught the basic physician leadership skills to play this role. And I failed—more than once! I adopted a leadership style based on giving orders not because I was hungry for power but because it seemed to work with the clinical actions of diagnosis and treatment. When faced with a clinical challenge, I assumed that I needed to come up with the answers (diagnose) and then tell everyone on the team what to do (treat).

Whenever I met a difficult challenge well—made a tough diagnosis or came up with a creative treatment plan for a difficult patient dilemma—my self-esteem went up. I developed a high level of confidence in my abilities. This was good progress, but it only went so far, as I started to believe (falsely) that I was solely responsible for these successes. I failed to recognize that despite some of my great ideas, a broader team was clearly involved in designing and implementing any successful patient plan.

At the time I didn't have the same level of self-awareness that I do now. I couldn't recognize my poor leadership behavior as a human limitation, one that anyone with some measure of success could fall prey to. I believed I was somehow superior simply because I performed my individual role well. As you might imagine, this had significant negative consequences for me. Although I was totally dedicated to my work and tirelessly served patients to the best of my abilities, my leadership style led to interpersonal conflicts, which limited my ability to be truly successful in this professional setting. It wasn't until I adopted a more collaborative and team-centered leadership style that I saw a big difference in my overall effectiveness.

How did I make this change? First and foremost I had the desire to change. That is something you must always find within yourself and acknowledge. Second, I had adopted yoga and used it to support this evolution in my leadership style. These efforts helped me develop a solid foundation for optimizing my leadership. I continually looked for ways to integrate my yoga into a more robust leadership style. I developed new skill sets by engaging in coaching, mentoring, and three intensive leadership development programs over a twelve-year period. None of this came easily, and I still occasionally slip back into old habits.

But I have grown. My leadership style has depth, breadth, and passion. I developed greater self-awareness, resilience, and clarity of mind, which allowed me to see things as they were (ineffective) without self-judgment. I developed improved flexibility not only in my physical body but also in my way of thinking. I enhanced my self-confidence. I developed dimensions of silence, consciousness, and appreciation in my daily life.

I'm very proud of my transformation, and I encourage you to embark on your own journey of enlightened leadership. To start this journey, first and foremost you must know yourself. As an enlightened leader you must be self-aware and understand your strengths and limitations, passions, and purpose. Enlightened leaders have a keen sense of both responsibility and personal freedom, and they feel gratitude for the opportunity to serve others.

Enlightened Leaders Are Committed to Making the World a Better Place

Here are twelve prominent characteristics of enlightened leaders:

1. **Compassionate.** Enlightened leaders understand the needs of others and put them above their own.

2. **Competent.** Enlightened leaders understand their strengths and can acknowledge their weaknesses. They are continually learning and evolving.

3. **Courageous.** Enlightened leaders have a strong sense of duty and are not afraid to go against the status quo.

4. **Humble.** Enlightened leaders are secure in their identity and lead without arrogance. They value the opinions and contributions of others and seek their engagement.

5. **Intentional.** Enlightened leaders take deliberate action to communicate their vision and mission. They take ownership of their decisions, regardless of whether they succeed or fail.

6. **Open-minded.** Enlightened leaders can see things from different perspectives. They are open to the beliefs and ideas of others.

7. **Passionate.** Enlightened leaders have a strong passion for their work. They put their heart and soul into it and are deeply committed through all circumstances, even the most difficult ones.

8. **Purposeful.** Enlightened leaders influence others through their deep sense of purpose and promote an ethical value system to foster an organizational culture with meaning.

9. **Self-aware.** Enlightened leaders have an awareness of themselves and others, are tuned in to their emotional state, and recognize how their actions are perceived by others.

10. **Self-caring.** Enlightened leaders practice self-care so that they are best able to lead others. They also encourage self-care for those they lead.

11. **Spiritual.** Enlightened leaders contemplate the principles of their own faith and lead with altruism, hope, and a commitment to make a difference in the lives of others.

12. **Visionary.** Enlightened leaders ask: How can I make the world a better place? Their vision is focused on people and helping to make a better world.

Self-Reflection

1. What are your passions, and are you pursuing them?

2. When have you achieved a flow state? What were you engaged in at the time?

3. Is your life fresh and full of joy every day?

4. What is your life purpose?

5. What are three things you can do each day to practice samadhi?

6. What are key characteristics of enlightened leaders?

7. What steps do you need to take to become an enlightened leader? Which one can you take today?

Conclusion

Steady for the Long Haul

"If your actions inspire others to dream more, learn
more, do more and become more, you are a leader."
—John Quincy Adams, sixth president of the United States

Yoga has offered me the strength, focus, tolerance, and discipline to effectively manage corporate uncertainties and to be an effective leader at
a time when change is the only constant. It has taught me how to influence others, cultivate strong relationships, and communicate effectively—all essential skills for leaders.

In the fall of 1993, very early in my career, I went on a group bicycle
trip through the hills of northern Vermont. Several days into the
trip it began raining fairly hard, but not wanting to miss an opportunity to ride, I put on my rain gear and continued on my bike journey.
Suddenly my bike skidded going uphill on the wet pavement. I could
not keep the bike upright, nor could I unlock my shoes from the

pedals, so I fell backward, landing on my left shoulder and wrenching my neck, with the bike on top of me. Help came immediately (other die-hards who were riding too stopped abruptly). I was able to stand up after they released me from the bike, seemingly unscathed. But gradually, over the next several days, I developed severe pain in my neck, with numbness and tingling down my left arm and hand that would not go away. (Needless to say, I did not ride for the remaining few days of the trip.)

I ended up in a neurosurgeon's office, and an MRI showed a cervical disc herniation, which explained my pain and numbness. However, the test also revealed a small, dense lesion in the anterior of my neck in the thyroid gland. I was told this was sure to be "nothing" but it would be best to biopsy this lesion, as I might need surgery to repair the disc herniation, so it was important to confirm whether the lesion was indeed "nothing."

It wasn't. The lesion was cancerous. Suddenly and unexpectedly I was a cancer patient. In three weeks I would undergo a complete thyroidectomy (my entire thyroid gland was removed) and radioactive iodine treatment to destroy any residual thyroid tissue not removed during the surgery.

We never know what our next moment holds.

Each person who has cancer has a unique story and undergoes an individual journey. Although I am an oncologist, I have actually struggled with both my cancer diagnosis and with identifying as a cancer survivor. Yet I *am* a cancer survivor. Although I did not undergo chemotherapy or external beam radiation (I had stage-one papillary carcinoma of the thyroid), this cancer has affected the entire course of my life. How? My voice. The breathing tube placed during the surgery irritated my larynx. I experienced bleeding in my neck shortly thereafter and found myself very hoarse. I seemed to experience almost all the complications that the doctor had advised might happen!

Months later, when the hoarseness did not go away, I went to an otolaryngologist who specialized in voice disorders and found that one of the nerves to my vocal cords had been damaged during the surgery and that my vocal cords did not move normally. Subsequently I had many rounds of speech therapy to help me to try to speak normally and to overcome chronic hoarseness. In recent years this problem has become more difficult for me, as I have experienced long-term dryness from the radioactive iodine—reduced tear formation, dry mouth, and dry vocal cords. Because the vocal folds need to be lubricated with a thin layer of mucus to vibrate efficiently, I must ensure proper voice care at all times and am rarely without a bottle of water that I sip all day.

What does this story have to do with yoga and leadership? Let's fast-forward twenty-four years since my diagnosis.

My favorite part of my job is to influence, educate, and lead through public forums. I am a good orator and believe that this type of platform gives me the best opportunity to reach people and to share what I have learned with others. Although I certainly found my niche, this type of role requires me to use my voice a lot—which is a challenge, given my diagnosis and lingering side effects. Every time I lead a meeting or give a speech, not only am I concerned about content and delivery, but I also fear that the quality of my voice will be poor and, in the worst circumstance, that I will lose my voice.

The previous eight chapters discussed ways in which yoga can help us develop and mature our leadership capabilities. I actually use these yogic teachings every day and especially when I step on a stage or conduct high-stakes meetings. I could have decided, *Why bother?* and chosen a different path in medicine than one that requires perpetual public speaking. I recognize that the sound of my voice can either help me to connect with my audience or be a deadly distraction—to both me and my audience.

But the truth is that I love what I do. Both science and communication are essential to promoting and protecting the health of the public. My ability to communicate effectively has allowed me to form connections, influence decisions, inspire people, and motivate change. Nevertheless, I live with the reality that my voice disorder persists and is there for me to deal with daily. I am keenly aware that at any time it could worsen. The principles and practices of yoga support me in maintaining a foundation of courage and authenticity from which I live my life, approach my work, and accept my limitations.

We began our leadership journey by moving beyond the yoga mat to an understanding of the yamas and niyamas, yoga's ethical guidelines, laid out in the first two limbs of Patañjali's eightfold path. The five yamas—ahimsa (nonviolence), satya (truthfulness), asteya (nonstealing), brahmacharya (nonexcess), and aparigraha (nonpossessiveness, nongreed)—are self-regulating behaviors involving our interactions with other people and the world at large. The five niyamas—saucha (purity), santosha (contentment), tapas (self-discipline), svadhyaya (self-study), and ishvara pranidhana (devotion)—are personal practices that relate to our inner world. The yamas and niyamas are not esoteric concepts but fundamental ethical precepts that serve as a foundation for skillful leading and living. By practicing the yamas, social contracts, or restraints, you become more disciplined. You are more apt to treat others with kindness and respect, which fosters positive relations. Genuine leaders consider their actions and the ramifications of their actions on others prior to exercising their positional power. By practicing the niyamas, key personal observances, you cultivate good self-care and strength of character. Being a great leader starts with you.

The yoga asana practice, described in the third limb, supports improved strength, endurance, and flexibility, all of which are necessary qualities for leaders, both physically and mentally. A challenging yoga practice *on* the mat trains you in how to accept discomfort as part of a learning process. Continued practice will lead you to become more resilient *off* the mat so you are better able to adapt to environments with continual change and uncertainty—which seems to be most situations in our world at large these days. It will also help you become more flexible both in body and as a characteristic of your leadership. We all know that not everything goes as planned. We must often reevaluate and redirect our plans. Flexible leaders embrace new ideas and plans and can manage themselves and their teams in the face of change and uncertainty.

The yoga asana practice trains you to become an observer or witness who simply notices what is without judging. How? At any given moment our minds seem to focus on our flaws and imperfections. We constantly compare ourselves to others and judge ourselves. When I first started yoga I would be on my mat and upset when I could not do a pose well. This led to further upset and rigidity in my body. With the help of good teachers I gradually learned to simply observe my discontentment. I realized that no one except me, including the teacher, really cared whether I could do a pose. I was trying to conform to what I thought I should do and what I *assumed* others expected from me. Once I began to observe myself and my reactions to each situation, I found less frustration and more joy in my practice.

Great leadership stems from the perspective of this observer who is not caught up in his problems and feelings about them but rather able to shift perspectives. Such individuals are not only aware of their individual circumstances but also of the bigger picture. So next time you get on your mat don't beat yourself up when you fall out of a pose—simply observe, smile, and move on. It's okay—it's yoga.

The fourth limb, pranayama, or mastery of the breath, has been key in my personal journey. I typically do at least five minutes of slow, conscious, deep breathing each day. I must breathe correctly to maximize the quality of my voice, so I ensure that I breathe from my diaphragm and take deep breaths before I speak. I have learned many pranayama techniques, but the most important to remember is simply to breathe! How many of us forget to breathe completely? What do we do when stressed? Forget to breathe. Nervous? Forget to breathe. Breathing is one of the most important things we can do to help ourselves pause in challenging situations and avoid possibly saying or doing something we may regret later. Taking just one deep breath will help you keep your emotions in check. Slow, deep diaphragmatic breathing aids in disengaging from distracting thoughts and sensations, calms our nervous system, and helps modulate our stress response so we choose a more thoughtful, productive response. The rhythm and the depth of your breath directly affects the state of your mind and the health of your body. So next time your boss upsets you, you forget to save your document, or someone cuts you off in traffic—just breathe!

We live in a world where we are often overwhelmed by the cacophony of noise from coworker chitchat, to the traffic outside, or to our electronic devices, which are always *on*. Distractions surround us. Using pratyahara, the fifth limb, we make the conscious effort to draw our awareness away from the external world and outside stimuli. Attention can be both focused and selective. The practice of pratyahara supports our desire to focus attention and select relevant information from irrelevant information, allowing for conscious, nonreactive decision making. By clearing our minds of everything that is not right in front of us, we learn to be more present. If you are one of those people who wakes up and, before you even brush your teeth, worry about what you forgot to do yesterday or about the day ahead—projects, deadlines, a sick child home from school—realize that this thinking pattern leads to stress and anxiety. Or if you have a constant need to check your phone, respond to email, or watch the news on TV, know that you are supporting a life of distractions. The way out is pratyahara. Next time you wake up, appreciate the sounds of birds outside your window and the smell of morning coffee, and then notice how water from your shower feels as it touches your skin. Turn your phone off—or at least put it away—for an hour. You will undoubtedly feel lighter and more free. With this newfound freedom you can enjoy the present moment.

The sixth limb is dharana, or concentration. Patañjali explains concentration as the "binding of consciousness to a [single] spot." A primary task of leadership is to direct attention. To do so, leaders must learn to focus their attention. Our attention is constantly under siege in modern life. Whereas technology supports learning and enhances connectedness and collaboration, the expansion of the digital age has led to a chronically "on" and "plugged in" society. What task did you interrupt when you picked up this book and started to read this chapter? An inability to focus and sustain attention can impact your relationships, job performance, and, well, just about everything! Next time you are in a meeting or a conversation with a friend, put away all your devices and listen intently. You may be amazed at your ability to engage and focus. And when you find yourself working at the computer for hours at a time, take a break. Even short diversions from your task at hand can dramatically improve your ability to resume work in a more focused manner for a prolonged period of time.

This ability to focus all the mind's attention toward one thing is the foundation of the seventh limb, dhyana, or meditation. In today's typical corporate environment employees are often asked to do more with less, in a fast-paced environment, and with multiple projects and demands occurring all the time. The high stress levels resulting from this ongoing frenzy of activity can have a negative impact on your health, relationships, and productivity. Incorporating meditation into your life can help reduce stress, improve decision making, enhance creativity, and increase emotional resilience. Meditation supports inspirational leadership, which combines serenity, a strong presence, self-knowledge, and knowledge of others with an ability to make faster and more accurate decisions.

Meditation does not have to be a formal and very serious undertaking. Just try it. Wherever you are and whenever you choose. Even for one minute. Meditation won't give you instant gratification, but if practiced over a period of time it will help you become more aware and grounded in the present moment. Certainly you want to be present for your own life!

The eighth and final limb of the yoga sutras is samadhi, the highest stage in meditation, an experience of ultimate presence, true alertness. In a state of samadhi we experience total absorption in our work or leisure activity, a total connectedness with the subject at hand; things become effortless, and we have the perception of "frozen time." Athletes call this state "being in the zone." I myself have experienced samadhi during some of my speaking engagements. When it happens, despite the high stakes and generally large audience, my voice is clear. My diction is fluid, and I feel like I am outside of myself, listening along with the audience to an articulate flow of material I've never heard before, delivered in a way I never rehearsed. Breakthrough moments may herald the creation of new insights that I use to advance my thinking and subsequent work to a new level. A renewed confidence and energy sustains me for weeks to come. Samadhi is an achievable goal for all of us. In the yogic teachings of samadhi your sense of being you—of being a body and mind and identifying with your thoughts—will dissolve, and you will experience only consciousness, a state of pure awareness. If that's hard to grasp, in a more practical sense, you will be immersed in a peace beyond what you ever imagined, a state of bliss.

What is your leadership vision and your sense of your own unique leadership style? What are your goals for your future? Leading at the highest level—no matter what your position—requires a clear vision. Once you have that vision, you must create positive momentum toward your vision through intentional action. For those who value organizational life but find it difficult to tolerate at times, I view the adoption of these intentional practices as a way to lead ourselves and others with greater happiness and ease. By embracing the principles and practices of yoga you will be able to communicate more clearly and confidently, tap into your intuition, creatively and resourcefully solve problems, showcase others' skills, and approach your work and life with a positive energy that inspires.

It is my hope that the downstream impact and expansion of this work will help shift the corporate dynamic and allow more individuals to "stay in" rather than "get out" through effective self-leadership and the leadership of others.

Namaste. The leader within me salutes the leader within you.

Afterword

I wrote a significant portion of this book on Sanibel Island, Florida—a peaceful paradise I have frequented since I was a small child. The beauty, tranquility, naturalized beaches, and gentle waves of Sanibel promote an inner calm from which my creativity flows. After visiting the island at least annually for nearly forty years, I purchased a condominium on Sanibel in April 2017. It was one of my life's greatest dreams come true.

During the four months that have passed, I spent many hours writing there. Now, as I conclude my final editing and review of this book on September 10, 2017, in my Connecticut home, I am getting alerts with warnings that Hurricane Irma will rake southwest Florida with a catastrophic storm surge and destructive winds. I begin to panic, as I read in the weekend edition of the *New York Times* that Hurricane Irma is one of the strongest storms in American history. I fear the worst for my Sanibel home, and yet it's hard for me to stay away from my technology devices; I continue to seek out information for the next few hours, tracking the course of the storm. With each update, my anxiety, upset, and stress heighten. I fret so much that I begin to catastrophize.

Finally, I come to my senses and realize that dwelling on this situation will not alter the storm's course. We cannot stop a hurricane in its tracks. I switch gears and pull out my tool kit: the concepts and ideas I have presented in *Beyond the Mat*.

I accept that I have no control over the course or the magnitude of this storm. The outcome will in no way be impacted by whether I observe its path minute-to-minute or sit quietly and read a book. So, I accept the situation for what it is: scary, difficult, and potentially devastating for many. If we can't change a situation or an outcome, our best option is to accept it and to deal with it. My acceptance leads to less worry and stress (I feel more peaceful), greater appreciation and gratitude for what I do have (I am warm and dry with a roof over my head), and a more compassionate perspective (I begin to think of others impacted by the storm and think about the clothing and supplies I will be able to donate).

When we explore the opportunities and possibilities that come out of difficult circumstances, they become easier to accept. These challenging situations often become a fundamental part of our personal growth. I hope this book has offered you a useful framework for optimizing your own life journey. Just remember, you can incorporate yoga and its principles into your everyday life no matter how busy you are. It's worth it. It works.

Glossary of Sanskrit Terms

adho muka svanasana: Downward Facing Dog pose (see page 95).

ahimsa: Nonviolence, compassion.

aparigraha: To take only what is necessary.

asana: Posture.

Ashtanga yoga: "eight-limbed yoga"; a system developed by the ancient yogic sage Patañjali outlined in his yoga sutras.

asteya: Nonstealing.

bhujangasana: Cobra pose (see page 97).

brahmacharya: Control of the senses.

dharana: Concentration, focus, or flow.

dhyana: Meditation, attention, contemplation.

drishti: Focal point.

ishvara pranidhana: Devotion or surrender (to the divine).

nadi shodhana pranayama: Alternate nostril breathing.

namaste: There are many translations for this word. Literally, it translates from Sanskrit as "I bow to you"; another popular translation is, "The divine light in me acknowledges the divine light in you."

niyamas: Observances.

prana: Breath, life force.

pranayama: Rhythmic control of breath.

pratyahara: Withdrawal and freedom of the mind from the domination of the senses and external objects.

salabhasana: Locust pose (see page 98).

samadhi: A state of consciousness in which the individual becomes one with what they are experiencing.

santosha: Contentment.

satya: Truth.

saucha: Cleanliness, purification.

savasana: Corpse pose (see page 184 for Seated Savasana).

sohum: Ancient mantra meaning, "I am that," an affirmation that the individual self can identify with the essence of the universe.

sutra: Sanskrit word meaning, "string" or "thread." In Indian literary traditions it also refers to an aphorism or a collection of aphorisms in the form of a text.

svadhyaya: Self-study.

tadasana: Mountain pose (see page 93).

tapas: Self-restraint.

uttanasana: Standing Forward Bend pose (see page 94).

yamas: Universal moral commandments.

yoga: Patañjali's definition: "yogas chitta vritti nirodhah," which means, "yoga is the cessation of the fluctuations of the mind."

yogi: A practitioner of yoga; one who follows the teachings and philosophy of yoga.

Acknowledgments

While I prefer to work alone and in quietude, my writing of this book has been supported and influenced by many. I have a great sense of both gratitude and appreciation for everyone who shared their expertise, offered contributions, gave words of encouragement, or offered praise for the work that I now share with you.

David Moldawer educated me on the publishing world and helped me to find the courage to move into this uncharted territory. Dave bolstered my confidence as a writer and remains a friend and trusted advisor.

Myrsini Stephanides, my literary agent, believed in me as a first-time author and stuck with me throughout the process. She has a remarkable skill set as an agent and a tireless dedication to her authors. Myrsini was a critical reader of my manuscript; she offered ongoing counsel and no-nonsense advice. I am deeply grateful for our ongoing partnership.

The entire team at Da Capo Press was terrific. Claire Schulz edited this book with finesse and meticulous attention to detail—she carefully considered every chapter, every paragraph, and every sentence. I admire her discipline and dedication. Every book goes through many revisions and edits. Claire ensured that my writing was on point for a diverse audience. She helped me to foster my creative potential as a writer and to develop and refine my literary voice. This book was further enhanced by the diligent efforts of Kevin Hanover, Matt Weston, Raquel Hitt, Josephine Mariea, and Lori Hobkirk.

The illustration on the book jacket and the interior figures were drawn by the remarkable, Samantha Hahn. I am deeply inspired by Samantha's stunning artwork and sense of style. The ethereal warrior image on the cover captures the composite of strength and grace that helps to define great leaders. The design of the book jacket was overseen by creative director, Alex Camlin, and supported by the talented team at Da Capo.

My yoga journey began nearly fifteen years ago. I have been taught by an amazing group of teachers representing diverse backgrounds in yoga. The director of my three-hundred-hour teacher training was Natasha Rizopoulos, a master instructor at Down Under Yoga, in Boston. She helped me to transform my knowledge, understanding, and appreciation of yoga. It was during this time that I cemented many of my ideas and initiated work in earnest on this book. I did so in the midst of what many would consider an insane schedule—working more than full time, traveling one weekend per month for an entire year from Connecticut to Boston for yoga training, incessantly reading about yoga philosophy and taking yoga classes, while doing my best to remain present for family and friends.

Teaching yoga is a labor of love. I have also had the privilege of learning from Heidi Sormaz, Barbara Ruzansky, Shankara Newton, Sarah Powers, David Swenson, Julie Gudmestad, Kate O'Donnell, Patricia Walden, Stephen Cope, Jurian Hughes, Ben Chused, Kate Heffernan, Elena Brower, Brian Kest, and Barbara Benagh. These individuals, with their diverse styles and perspectives, helped to inform my thinking and behaviors both on and off the mat.

No one is born a leader. Leadership is learned. Great leaders are typically ardent students of leadership—they solicit frank feedback from supervisors and peers and seek out coaches, mentors, and/or professional development programs in order to enhance their skills and performance. They push themselves beyond their comfort zone and are not afraid to accept new challenges. My leadership journey has been supported and enhanced by executive coach Marsha Clark. Marsha constructively challenged my thinking and approaches and helped me to expand my sense of what may be possible in my career. Ellen McCormick served as my professional mentor. Ellen helped me to effectively lead in a cost-conscious, complex, matrix corporate environment. She continually said that I could do anything I set my mind to. Ellen believed in me when others had doubts.

Having a cancer diagnosis has made me a better and more humble leader. Both healthy cancer survivorship and effective leadership require fortitude, perseverance, and resilience. And they both require support. I have undertaken my cancer journey surrounded and supported by many, although I occasionally feel isolated with my cancer-related challenges. For more than ten years Dr. Beatriz Olson has offered me an integrated approach to the long-term management of thyroid cancer and its related treatment effects. Dr. Linda Carroll has helped me manage a complex and chronic voice disorder. With diligent effort to voice care and adherence to a vocal exercise plan, I can successfully engage in activities that require public speaking with limited fear I will become hoarse, or worse, lose my voice completely.

I wrote this book wherever and whenever I could find protected space and time. My focus is sharp, and my writing flows best in peaceful and relaxed environments—places where I can take breaks and spend time in nature. I thank friends at the Woodstock Inn and Norman Williams library in Woodstock, Vermont, for sharing your facilities and wonderful community with me. I am also grateful for the help of Mark Sinibaldi, who ensured that I had optimal writing space in Sanibel Island, Florida, which is now my second home. Mark always gave words of encouragement, especially when things were tough, and I thank him for his dedication and for cheering me on.

A number of friends and colleagues offered support, friendship, partnership, and/or counsel as I pursued my work. Ben Horwitz, Iris Blasi, Ursula Cary, Jane Friedman, Jennifer Horowitz, Michael Friedman, and John Ciprus applauded my ambition and helped me get to the finish line.

My father, William Jay Katz, remains a voice of reason despite his untimely passing in 2007. My sister, Beth Ellen Katz, is always an inspiration, as she exudes positivity and resilience in the face of challenging circumstances. Finally, my son, Ryan Taylor Rosenberg, has helped me to find meaning, joy, and humor in life.

May we all lead and live with more laughter. In the words of Winston Churchill, "It is my belief, you cannot deal with the most serious things in the world unless you understand the most amusing."

References

A View on Buddhism. 2016. "Compassion and Bodhicitta." Retrieved from http://viewonbuddhism.org/compassion.html.

Acevedo, Bianca P., Sarah Pospos, and Helen Lavretsky. 2016. "The Neural Mechanism of Meditative Practices: Novel Approaches for Healthy Aging." *Current Behavioral Neuroscience Reports* 3.4 (2016): 328–339. Retrieved from http://news.harvard.edu/gazette/story/2011/01/eight-weeks-to-a-better-brain.

Amma. 2017. Retrieved from http://amma.org.

Andersen, Hans Christian. 2015. "The Emperor's New Clothers: A Translation." The Hans Christian Andersen Center. Retrieved from http://www.andersen.sdu.dk/vaerk/hersholt/TheEmperorsNewClothes_e.html.

Ansari, Azadeh. 2016. "Ryan Lochte: 'I Over-Exaggerated' Olympics Robbery Story." CNN, August 22. http://edition.cnn.com/2016/08/20/sport/us-olympics-swimmers-reported-robbery-future.

Anxiety Slayer. 2009. "Self Help Anxiety Tip: The Long Exhale." Retrieved from http://www.anxietyslayer.com/journal/self-help-anxiety-tip-the-long-exhale.html.

Becker, Joshua. 2017. "21 Surprising Statistics that Reveal How Much Stuff We Actually Own." Becoming Minimalist. Retrieved from www.becomingminimalist.com/clutter-stats.

Blinder, Alan. 2017. "Robert Bentley, Alabama Governor, Resigns Amid Scandal." *New York Times*, April 10. Retrieved from www.nytimes.com/2017/04/10/us/robert-bentley-alabama-governor.html.

Booe, Martin. 2017. "What Are the Benefits of Yoga in the Workplace?" Livestrong, February 16. Retrieved from http://www.livestrong.com/article/360372-what-are-the-benefits-of-yoga-in-the-workplace.

Bortoluz, Via Sara. 2016. "The Hidden Meaning of Silence—Insights from Japanese Buddhist Culture." *Elephant Journal*, July 5. Retrieved from http://www.elephantjournal.com/2016/07/the-hidden-meaning-of-silence-insights-from-japanese-buddhist-culture.

Brafford, Anne. 2016. "Five Ways to Enhance Your Happiness: Way #2—Finding Your Mojo at Work." Aspire, August 19. Retrieved from http://aspire.legal/blog/five-ways-to-enhance-your-happiness-way-2finding-your-mojo-at-work.

Bratskelr, Kate. 2015. "Why You Should Do Yoga with Your Dog, and How to Start." *Huffington Post*, August 7.

Brennan-Cressey, Shannon. 2017. "10 Benefits of Practicing Yoga at Work." GeekHive, March 2. Retrieved from http://www.geekhive.com/buzz/post/2017/03/10-benefits-of-practicing-yoga-at-work.

Buchanan, Leigh. 2016. "Why This Company's Mission Includes No-Meeting Mondays." *Inc.*, May. Retrieved from http://www.inc.com/magazine/201605/leigh-buchanan/toms-employee-culture-programs.html.

Center for Healthy Minds. 2017. University of Wisconsin-Madison. Retrieved from https://centerhealthyminds.org.

Chappell, Bill. 2016. "Ryan Lochte Apologizes for 'Not Being More Careful and Candid' in Rio." NPR, August 18. Retrieved from http://www.npr.org/sections/thetorch/2016/08/19/490624710/ryan-lochte-apologizes-for-not-being-more-careful-and-candid.

Chopra, Manish. 2016. "Want to Be a Better Leader? Observe More and React Less." *McKinsey Quarterly*, February. Retrieved from http://www.mckinsey.com/global-themes/leadership/want-to-be-a-better-leader-observe-more-and-react-less.

Coffey, Wayne. 2005. *The Boys of Winter: The Untold Story of a Coach, a Dream, and the 1980 U.S. Olympic Hockey Team*. New York: Random House.

Csikszentmihalyi, Mihaly. 2008. *Flow: The Psychology of Optimal Experience*. New York: Harper & Row.

Cuddy, Amy. 2015. *Presence: Bringing Your Boldest Self to Your Biggest Challenges* New York: Little, Brown.

David, Susan. 2016. *Emotional Agility: Get Unstuck, Embrace Change, and Thrive in Work and Life*. New York: Avery Publishing Group.

DiSalvo, David. 2013. "Breathing and Your Brain: Five Reasons to Grab the Controls." *Forbes*, May 14. Retrieved from http://www.forbes.com/sites/daviddisalvo/2013/05/14/breathing-and-your-brain-five-reasons-to-grab-the-controls/#437e26502d95.

Drucker, Peter F. 2005. "Managing Oneself." *Harvard Business Journal*, January. Retrieved from https://hbr.org/2005/01/managing-oneself.

Easwaran, Eknath. 2010. *The Bhagavad Gita*. Ahmedabad: Jaico Publishing House.

Edelman.com. 2016. "2016 Edelman Trust Barometer." Retrieved from http://www.edelman.com/insights/intellectual-property/2016-edelman-trust-barometer.

eDiplomat. 2017. "Japan." Retrieved from http://www.ediplomat.com/np/cultural_etiquette/ce_jp.htm.

Field, Tiffany. 2016. "Yoga Research Review." *Complementary Therapies in Clinical Practice* 24 (August): 145–161.

Freudenberger, Herbert. 1974. "Staff Burn-Out." *Journal of Social Issues* 30.1: 159–165.

Gandhi, Mahatma. 2012. *The Bhagavad Gita According to Gandhi: Introduction, Text and Commentary Translated from Gujarati*. Delhi: Orient Publishing.

Gelles, David. 2013. "5 Ways to Stay Happy + Healthy at Work." *Yoga Journal*, July 31. Retrieved from http://www.yogajournal.com/lifestyle/all-in-a-day-s-work.

Gelles, David. 2015. "At Aetna, a C.E.O.'s Management by Mantra." *New York Times*, February 27. Retrieved from http://www.nytimes.com/2015/03/01/business/at-aetna-a-ceos-management-by-mantra.html?_r=0.

George, Bill. 2015. *Discover Your True North*. Hoboken, NJ: Wiley.

Ginsburg, Ruth Bader. 2016. "Ruth Bader Ginsburg's Advice for Living." *New York Times*, October 1. Retrieved from www.nytimes.com/2016/10/02/opinion/sunday/ruth-bader-ginsburgs-advice-for-living.html.

Goetz, Jennifer. 2004. "Research on Buddhist Conceptions of Compassion: An Annotated Bibliography." *Greater Good Magazine*, June 1. Retrieved from https://test-greatergood.berkeley.edu/article/item/buddhist_conceptions_of_compassion_an_annotated_bibliography.

Goldsmith, Marshall. 2010. *Mojo: How to Get It, How to Keep It, How to Get It Back If You Lose It*. New York: Hyperion.

Goldsmith, Marshall. 2014. *What Got You Here Won't Get You There: How Successful People Become Even More Successful!* New York: Hyperion.

Goldstein, Elisha. 2013. "Stressing Out? S.T.O.P." *Mindful*, May 29. Retrieved from http://www.mindful.org/stressing-out-stop.

Goleman, Daniel. 2013. *Focus: The Hidden Driver of Excellence*. New York: HarperCollins.

Goodman, Peter S. 2013. "Why Companies Are Turning to Meditation and Yoga to Boost the Bottom Line." *Huffington Post*, July 11. Retrieved from http://www.huffingtonpost.com/2013/07/11/mindfulness-capitalism_n_3572952.html.

Goudreau, Jenna. 2011. "Is Office Clutter Costing You a Promotion?" *Forbes*, January 31. Retrieved from http://www.forbes.com/sites/jenna

goudreau/2011/01/31/is-office-clutter-costing-you-a-promotion
-organize-hoard-enough-already-peter-walsh-own/#30b2ec9e4046.

Hall, Alena. 2015. "A Compassionate Work Culture Can Really Benefit
the Bottom Line, Too." *Huffington Post*, April 29. Retrieved from
http://www.huffingtonpost.com/2015/04/29/compassion-at-work
_n_7057382.html.

Halpern, Jake. 2013. "Amma's Multifaceted Empire, Built on Hugs." *New
York Times*, May 25. Retrieved from http://www.nytimes.com/2013
/05/26/business/ammas-multifaceted-empire-built-on-hugs.html
?mtrref=www.google.
com&gwh=7DE1FE239FBFED6DB6128B1357B4B60F&gwt=pay.

Halvorson, Heidi Grant. 2011. "How to Give Employees a Sense of Autonomy (when You Are Really Calling the Shots)" *Forbes*, September
15. Retrieved from http://www.forbes.com/sites/heidigranthalvorson
/2011/09/15/how-to-give-employees-a-sense-of-autonomy-when
-you-are-really-calling-the-shots/#5a5ac83477c6.

Harris, Dan. 2014. *10% Happier: How I Tamed the Voice in My Head, Reduced Stress Without Losing My Edge, and Found Self-Help that Actually
Works—A True Story*. London: Yellow Kite.

Harter, Jim. 2014. "Should Employers Ban Email After Work Hours?"
Gallup, *Business Journal*, September 9. Retrieved from http://www
.gallup.com/businessjournal/175670/employers-ban-email-work-hours
.aspx.

Howard, Jacqueline. 2016. "Americans Devote More than 10 Hours a Day
to Screen Time, and Growing." CNN, July 29. Retrieved from http://
www.cnn.com/2016/06/30/health/americans-screen-time-nielsen.

Information Overload Research Group (IORG). 2017. "About IORG."
Retrieved from http://iorgforum.org/about-iorg.

Iyengar, B. K. S. 2016. *Light on Prānāyāma: The Yogic Art of Breathing*. New
York: Crossroad Publishing Company.

Jaworski, Joseph. 2011. *Synchronicity: The Inner Path of Leadership*. Santa
Francisco: Berrett-Koehler Publishers.

Jinpa, Thupten. 2016. *A Fearless Heart: How the Courage to Be Compassionate Can Transform Our Lives*. Garden City Park, NY: Avery Publishing Group.

Keller, Doug. 2003. *Refining the Breath: The Yogic Practice of Pranayama*. South Riding, VA: Do Yoga Productions.

Ken Blanchard Companies. 2017. "People-Centered Leadership." Retrieved from http://www.kenblanchard.com/KBCPublic/media/PDF/People-Centered-Leadership-eBook-mk0806.pdf.

Kilpatrick, Carroll. 1974. "Nixon Resigns." *Washington Post*, August 9. Retrieved from http://www.washingtonpost.com/wp-srv/national/longterm/watergate/articles/080974-3.htm.

Klein, Asher. 2015. "Pope Francis's 1st U.S. Popemobile Is a Fiat." 4 New York, September 22. Retrieved from http://www.nbcnewyork.com/news/national-international/Pope-Francis-Popemobile-Washington-Fiat-328713901.html.

Kondo, Marie. 2011. *The Life-Changing Magic of Tidying Up: The Japanese Art of Decluttering and Organizing*. North Charleston, SC: Create Space Independent Publishing.

Kondo, Marie. 2016. *Spark Joy: An Illustrated Master Class on the Art of Organizing and Tidying Up*. Berkeley, CA: Ten Speed Press.

Langewiesche, William. 2010. *Fly by Wire: The Geese, the Glide, the Miracle on the Hudson*. London: Picador.

Lee, Kate E., Kathryn J. H. Williams, Leisa D. Sargent, Nicholas S. G. Williams, Katherine A. Johnson. 2015. "40-Second Green Roof Views Sustain Attention: The Role of Micro-Breaks in Attention Restoraion." *Journal of Environmental Psychology* 42 (June): 182–189.

Lesser, Marc. 2016. "Take Care of the Work; Take Care of Yourself—Search Inside Yourself Engage." *Huffington Post*, March 3. Retrieved from http://www.huffingtonpost.com/marc-lesser/take-care-of-the-work-tak_b_9372714.html.

Lickona, Thomas. 2017. "Prevent Peer Cruelty and Promote Kindness." Catholic Education Resource Center. Retrieved from http://www .catholiceducation.org/en/education/catholic-contributions/prevent -peer-cruelty-and-promote-kindness.html.

Livingston, Jennifer A. 1997. "Metacognition: An Overview." Retrieved from http://gse.buffalo.edu/fas/shuell/cep564/metacog.htm.

Maloney, Alli. 2015. "How Ruth Bader Ginsburg Became 'Notorious R.B.G..'" Women in the World. Retrieved from http://nytlive.nytimes .com/womenintheworld/2015/11/03/ how-ruth-bader-ginsburg-became-notorious-r-b-g.

Manville, Brook. 2015. "Is It OK for Leaders to Lie?" *Forbes*, November 15. Retrieved from http://www.forbes.com/sites/brookmanville /2015/11/15/is-it-ok-for-leaders-to-lie/#56f9d96563a4.

Marquis, Christopher, and Andrew Park. 2014. "Inside the Buy-One Give-One Model." Stanford Social Innovation Review (Winter): 28–33. Retrieved from http://www.people.hbs.edu/cmarquis/inside _the_buy_one_give_one_model.pdf.

Marshall, Linda. 2011. "From Granny's Store to G. M." *New York Times*, October 15. Retrieved from http://www.nytimes.com/2011/10/16 /jobs/16boss.html.

McCall, Timothy. 2007. "38 Health Benefits of Yoga." *Yoga Journal*, August 28. Retrieved from http://www.yogajournal.com/lifestyle /count-yoga-38-ways-yoga-keeps-fit.

McGuckin, Amber. 2017. "Manitoba Petting Farm Getting in on Goat Yoga Craze." *Global News*, April 21. Retrieved from http://globalnews .ca/news/3394559/manitoba-petting-farm-getting-in-on-goat-yoga -craze.

McNamara, Alix, with Caroling Howard. 2016. "The World's 100 Most Powerful Women." *Forbes*, June 6. Retrieved from http://www.forbes .com/power-women.

Mind, Body and Spirit Wellbeing. 2016. "The Amazing Benefits of Dia-
    phragmatic Breathing." Retrieved from http://mindbodyandspirit
    wellbeing.com/diaphragmatic-breathing-benefits.

Monster.com. 2014. "Dangerously Stressful Work Environments Force
    Workers to Seek New Employment." April 16. Retrieved from http://
    www.monster.com/about/a/dangerously-stressful-work-environments
    -force-workers-to-seek-new-empl4162014-d3126696.

Napier, Nancy K. 2014. "The Myth of Multitasking." *Psychology Today*,
    May 12. Retrieved from http://www.psychologytoday.com/blog
    /creativity-without-borders/201405/the-myth-multitasking.

Navy. 2017. "Combat Tactical Breathing." Retrieved from http://www
    .med.navy.mil/sites/nmcphc/Documents/health-promotion-wellness
    /psychological-emotional-wellbeing/Combat-Tactical-Breathing.pdf.

Nelson, Patrick. 2016. "We Touch Our Phones 2,617 Times a Day, Says
    Study." Network World, July 7. Retrieved from http://www.network
    world.com/article/3092446/smartphones/we-touch-our-phones-2617
    -times-a-day-says-study.html.

Neupert, Geoff. 2014. "The Most Important Exercise Missing from
    Your Workout." *Men's Health*, October 29. Retrieved from http://
    www.menshealth.com/fitness/diaphragmatic-breathing.

Nguyen, Steve. 2016. "Cost of Stress on the U.S. Economy Is $300 Bil-
    lion? Says Who?" Workplace Psychology, July 4. Retrieved from
    https://workplacepsychology.net/2016/07/04/cost-of-stress-on-the
    -u-s-economy-is-300-billion-says-who.

Novotny, Sarah, and Len Kravitz. 2017. "The Science of Breathing."
    University of New Mexico. Retrieved from http://www.unm.edu
    /~lkravitz/Article%20folder/Breathing.html.

Oliver, Joan Duncan. 2009. "Buddha in the Googleplex." Tricycle, Sum-
    mer 2009. Retrieved from https://tricycle.org/magazine/buddha
    -googleplex.

Patañjali. 1985. *The Yoga Sutras of Patañjali*. Translated by Sri Swami
    Satchidananda. Yogaville, VA: Integral Yoga Publications.

Perciavalle, Valentina, Marta Blandini, Paola Fecarotta, Andrea Buscemi, Donatalla Di Corrado, Luana Bertolo, Fulvia Fichera, and Marinella Coco. 2017. "The Role of Deep Breathing on Stress." *Neurological Science* 38.3 (March): 451–458.

Quittner, Jeremy. 2016. "What the Founder of TOMS Shoes Is Doing Now." *Fortune*, September 8. Retrieved from http://fortune.com/2016/09/08/what-the-founder-of-toms-shoes-is-doing-now.

Rogers, Bruce. 2016. "Tech Titan Jim Goodnight Positions SAS for the Future." *Forbes*, October 31. Retrieved from http://www.forbes.com/sites/brucerogers/2016/10/31/tech-titan-jim-goodnight-positions-sas-for-the-future/#7b6fbdad4e55.

Rosenfield, Mark. 2011. "Computer Vision Syndrome: A Review of Ocular Causes and Potential Treatments." *Ophthalmic and Physiological Optics* 31.5: 502–515.

Sana, Faria, Tina Weston, and Nicholas J. Cepeda. 2013. "Laptop Multitasking Hinders Classroom Learning for Both Users and Nearby Peers." *Computers and Education* 62 (March): 24–31.

Schmerler, Jessica. 2015. "Q&A: Why Is Blue Light Before Bedtime Bad for Sleep?" *Scientific American*, September 1. Retrieved from http://www.scientificamerican.com/article/q-a-why-is-blue-light-before-bedtime-bad-for-sleep.

Science Daily. 2011. "Brief Diversions Vastly Improve Focus, Researchers Find." February 8. Retrieved from http://www.sciencedaily.com/releases/2011/02/110208131529.htm.

Search Inside Yourself Leadership Institute. 2017. Retrieved from https://siyli.org.

Seidman, Bianca. 2015. "What Too Much Screen Time Does to Your Eyes." CBS News, August 13. Retrieved from http://www.cbsnews.com/news/screen-time-digital-eye-strain.

Sheridan, Jerry. 2011. "Tactical Breathing Can Stop Stress on the Spot." On Resilience, June 2. Retrieved from http://onresilience.com/2011/06/02/tactical-breathing-can-stop-stress-on-the-spot.

Sinek, Simon. 2009. *Start with Why: How Great Leaders Inspire Everyone to Take Action.* New York: Portfolio/Penquin.

Skaugset, L. Melissa, Susan Farrell, Michele Carney, Margaret Wolff, and Sally A. Santen. 2016. "Can You Multitask? Evidence and Limitations of Task Switching and Multitasking in Emergency Medicine." *Annals of Emergency Medicine* 68.2 (August): 189–195.

SmartLife Push Journal, http://www.smartlifepushjournal.com.

Spira, Jonathan. 2001. *Overload! How Too Much Information Is Hazardous to Your Organization.* Hoboken, NJ: John Wiley & Sons.

Sravani. 2017. "21 Vital Factors that Influence Employees Job Satisfaction." Wisestep. Retrieved from http://content.wisestep.com/vital-factors-that-influence-employees-job-satisfaction.

Stallard, Michale Lee. 2010. "Has Jim Goodnight Cracked the Code of Corporate Culture?" June 18. Retrieved from http://www.michaelleestallard.com/has-jim-goodnight-cracked-the-code-of-corporate-culture.

Stewart, James B. 2016. "Facebook Has 50 Minutes of Your Time Each Day. It Wants More." *New York Times*, May 6. Retrieved from http://www.nytimes.com/2016/05/06/business/facebook-bends-the-rules-of-audience-engagement-to-its-advantage.html.

Stone, Linda. 2012. "The Connected Life: From Email Apnea to Conscious Computing." *Huffington Post*, July 7. Retrieved from http://www.huffingtonpost.com/linda-stone/email-apnea-screen-apnea-_b_1476554.html.

Stone, Linda. 2014. "Are You Breathing? Do You Have Email Apnea?" November 24. Retrieved from https://lindastone.net/2014/11/24/are-you-breathing-do-you-have-email-apnea;

Tan, Chade-Meng. 2010. "Everyday Compassion at Google." TED, November. Retrieved from http://www.ted.com/talks/chade_meng_tan_everyday_compassion_at_google.

Tan, Chade-Meng. 2014. *Search Inside Yourself: The Unexpected Path to Achieving Success, Happiness (and World Peace)*. New York: Harper One.

The Art of Living. 2017. "Benefits of Meditation." Retrieved from http://www.artofliving.org/us-en/meditation/benefits-of-meditation.

Tjan, Anthony K. 2012. "How Leaders Become Self-Aware." *Harvard Business Review*, July 19. Retrieved from https://hbr.org/2012/07/how-leaders-become-self-aware.

Trotman, Andrew. 2014. "Facebook's Mark Zuckerberg: Why I Wear the Same T-Shirt Every Day." *Telegraph*, November 7. Retrieved from http://www.telegraph.co.uk/technology/facebook/11217273/Facebooks-Mark-Zuckerberg-Why-I-wear-the-same-T-shirt-every-day.html.

USA Hockey. 2015. "Miracle." Retrieved from http://www.usahockey.com/miracle.

Washington Post. 2004. "Transcript: Illinois Senate Candidate Barack Obama." July 27. Retrieved from http://www.washingtonpost.com/wp-dyn/articles/A19751-2004Jul27.html.

Williams, Ray. 2012. "Why We Need Kind and Compassionate Leaders." *Psychology Today*, August 28. Retrieved from http://www.psychologytoday.com/blog/wired-success/201208/why-we-need-kind-and-compassionate-leaders.

Willingham, A. J. 2017. "'Goat Yoga' Is a Thing—and Hundred Are Lining Up for It." CNN, January 12.

Winerman, Lea. 2013. "A Messy Desk Encourages a Creative Mind, Study Finds." *Monitor on Psychology* 44.9 (October): 12. Retrieved from www.apa.org/monitor/2013/10/messy-desk.aspx.

Woollaston, Victoria. 2015. "How Often Do YOU Check Your Phone? Average User Picks Up Their Devide 85 Times a DAY—Twice as Often as They Realize." *Daily Mail*, October 29. Retrieved from http://

www.dailymail.co.uk/sciencetech/article-3294994/How-check-phone
    -Average-user-picks-device-85-times-DAY-twice-realise.html.
Workplace Evolved. 2017. "Why Corporate Yoga?" Retrieved from http://
    www.workplaceevolved.com/wellness-programs/workplace-yoga/why
    -corporate-yoga.
Yoga Journal. 2007. "Channel-Cleaning Breath." August 28. Retrieved
    from http://www.yogajournal.com/poses/channel-cleaning-breath.
Yoga Journal. 2016. "2016 Yoga in America Study Conducted by Yoga
    Journal and Yoga Alliance." Retrieved from http://www.yogajournal
    .com/yogainamericastudy.
Zetlin, Minda. 2014. "Why Pope Francis Is So Effective: 8 Lessons for
    Every Leader." *Inc.*, August 1. Retrieved from http://www.inc.com
    /minda-zetlin/why-pope-francis-is-so-effective-8-lessons-for-every
    -leader.html.

Index

About the Author

Julie Rosenberg, MD, is a physician executive who has worked in a variety of leadership roles in the pharmaceutical industry. She has actively practiced yoga for more than fifteen years and completed both 200- and 300-hour yoga teacher trainings. Dr. Rosenberg teaches yoga primarily "beyond the mat," helping individuals and groups apply the principles and practice of yoga to their daily lives to support their overall health and well-being, to achieve success, and to become more effective leaders. She lives in Connecticut and Florida. Find out more on the web at www.julierosenbergmd.com.